CAN YOU TRUST YOUR TRUST?

What You Need to Know about the Advantages and Disadvantages of Trusts and Trust Compliance Issues

SEYMOUR GOLDBERG
CPA, MBA, JD

Cover design by Elmarie Jara/ABA Publishing.

18 17 16 15 14 5 4 3 2 1

Library of Congress Cataloging-in-Publication Data

Goldberg, Seymour, author.
  Can you trust your trust? / Seymour Goldberg.
     p. cm.
  Includes bibliographical references and index.
  1. Trusts and trustees--United States. I. Title.
  KF730.G65 2014
  346.7305'9--dc23

                                   2014028871

Discounts are available for books ordered in bulk. Special consideration is given to state bars, CLE programs, and other bar-related organizations. Inquire at Book Publishing, ABA Publishing, American Bar Association, 321 N. Clark Street, Chicago, Illinois 60654-7598.

www.ShopABA.org

Contents

About the Author

SEYMOUR GOLDBERG, CPA, MBA, JD, is a senior partner in the law firm of Goldberg & Goldberg, PC, in Woodbury, New York. He is professor emeritus of law and taxation at Long Island University. Mr. Goldberg is the recipient of the American Jurisprudence Award in Federal Estate and Gift Taxation from St. John's University School of Law. As an instructor for the Foundation for Accounting Education and the American Institute of Certified Public Accountants, Mr. Goldberg has taught many CPE courses in taxation and trust accounting at the state and national levels and has taught CLE courses for the New York State Bar Association, local bar associations, and law schools. He is the recipient of outstanding discussion leader awards from both the American Institute of Certified Public Accountants and the Foundation for Accounting Education. He was formerly associated with the Internal Revenue Service. Mr. Goldberg has been quoted in the *New York Times, Forbes, Fortune, Money Magazine, U.S. News & World Report, Business Week, The Wall Street Journal*, and the *Tax Hotline*. He has also been interviewed on CNN, CNBC, and WCBS. Mr. Goldberg has also served as a member of the IRS Long Island Tax Practitioner Liaison Committee and the Northeast Pension Liaison Group. He has been involved in conducting continuing education outreach programs with the IRS. Mr. Goldberg has authored manuals for the American Bar Association, American Institute of Certified Public Accountants, and other organizations.

Overview

This book is written because of the expanding use of trusts in this country. A trust is frequently looked at as the alter ego of a will. Trusts are often worthwhile but can be a devastating nightmare if they are administered improperly. Unfortunately, trust litigation is expanding, and challenges to the actions of trustees by beneficiaries are the subject of continuing education programs by the American Bar Association and other bar associations.

As a result of the revamping of state trust laws in many states, trustees will find themselves with headaches. This guide will advise you on the benefits as well as the pitfalls of acting as a trustee.

Author's Note

Throughout this book, there is reference to the Uniform Principal and Income Act (UPAIA) and the Uniform Trust Code (UTC). The states can adopt these uniform acts, which control to a major extent the rules that apply to the administration of trusts that are governed by a particular state's trust law.

Most states have adopted versions of the UPAIA with various effective dates. A number of states have adopted versions of the UTC with various effective dates as well.

The UPAIA covers the determination of what is income and what is principal under the state trust law for trust accounting purposes. For the most part, these rules do not follow the IRS income tax rules.

The UTC covers many technical issues that come up in the administration of a trust other than the trust accounting income and principal rules.

TRUSTEE HEADACHES IN GENERAL

Being selected as a trustee is considered by many to be both an honor and a privilege. It also means authority and power. Obviously, any discretion delegated to a trustee must be exercised in a proper manner and in an impartial way. Naturally, holding the position of a trustee will also result in trustee commissions to the trustee.

The problems facing a trustee may take place in a silent and strange way. As an author, I have found that trustees face unforeseen difficulties. In many instances, the difficulties are thrust upon the trustee without the trustee's knowledge.

One point that must be emphasized is the need for the trustee to read the trust instrument. The trust document may be five pages long or 50 pages long. In any event, the document must be read and understood.

I suggest that the individual trustee should read the trust document several times and then have it explained by a knowledgeable trust attorney.

Often, the trustee looks at the trust document and may not fully understand the provisions it contains. If the trustee does not follow the terms of the trust document, then he or she has made a first mistake. This mistake can subject the trustee to problems with the trust beneficiaries at a later date.

CHANGING TRUST LAWS

Perhaps the next headache for a trust is the fact that there are periodic revisions of the state trust laws that often clarify, expand, or change the obligations of a trustee. Unfortunately, many trustees are not experts in trust law and may not know that the trust laws in their state have changed. The trustee may be a successful businessperson or professional, but he or she may not have the time or the inclination to study the trust document or meet with a trust attorney from time to time to determine his or her trustee obligations. Many trust documents are extremely complex.

In general, once the trust is activated, the trustee tends to go it alone and assumes that the state trust laws remain constant. However, state trust laws do not remain constant. In addition, the courts are constantly interpreting the meaning and the terms of trust documents, especially if the document is confusing and ambiguous.

Often, the trust beneficiaries haul the trustee into court because they feel that they have been shortchanged and treated unfairly.

Trust litigation and estate litigation is big business. Catching a sleepy and sloppy trustee on technical violations is not a difficult assignment for an experienced trust litigator.

A significant problem for a trustee exists when he or she relies on an adviser who may not know that the state trust laws have been changed or modified in the state that determines the interpretation of the trust's provisions.

Many states have adopted, for example, a revised version of the Uniform Principal and Income Act (UPAIA). These trust laws for the most part apply to existing trusts and newly formed trusts as well. The trust laws of the particular state must be checked in order to determine the effective date of the UPAIA in that particular state. The UPAIA defines how accounting income and principal are determined. It also explains how disbursements are treated and whether the disbursements are payable from income or principal. Other state trust laws often describe how certain trust disbursements are treated as well. The UPAIA defines certain receipts in a manner that is different from the normal definition of income. Whenever the word *state* is used in this manual, it includes the District of Columbia.

A suggested version of the UPAIA is initially drafted by the National Conference of Commissioners on Uniform State Laws. The states then consider whether to adopt the UPAIA in whole, in part, or not at all. Most states have adopted versions of the UPAIA with various effective dates. Periodically, the state modifies its existing trust accounting rules prospectively. This can be a nightmare if the trustee is not aware of the changes and operates under the old set of the trust accounting rules.

The UPAIA has a profound effect on a trust that states that the income from the trust must be paid to the income beneficiary of the trust since there are certain definitions regarding the determination of income under trust law. Income under trust law is not the same as income from an IRS point of view.

Some trusts provide that the trustee may distribute income each year to the income beneficiary, while other trusts provide that the trust beneficiary shall receive the income from the trust each year.

Which way the trust is drafted depends on the creator of the trust. If you are concerned that the income beneficiary may not be able to handle his or her affairs properly or have other concerns about that person, then a discretionary approach can be used. Alternatively, if you are concerned that the trustee may be too conservative in making discretionary income distributions to the income beneficiary, then you can provide that the income beneficiary shall receive the income from the trust each year. The trust may also provide for discretionary distributions of principal as well.

THE TRUSTEE AND STATE TRUST LAWS

Over the last decade or more, most states plus the District of Columbia have adopted versions of the 1997 UPAIA.

These revised laws triggered the need for the Tax Division of the American Institute of Certified Public Accountants (AICPA) in December 2007 to issue a comprehensive *Practice Guide for Fiduciary (Trust) Accounting*. It is a guide for accountants who perform fiduciary accounting services.

This practice guide (including the appendix) is over 250 pages long. The purpose is to provide information on what issues the CPA should know about when preparing fiduciary accountings and fiduciary income tax returns.

A dedicated number of members of the AICPA spent several years developing the trust accounting practice guide. These AICPA members were members of the AICPA Trust Accounting Income (TAI) Task Force.

In 2008, amendments were adopted by the National Conference of Commissioners on Uniform State Laws to the 1997 version of UPAIA. Each jurisdiction then decided whether or not to adopt the recommended changes in whole or in part. Most states have adopted the recommended changes, but a number of states did not. This makes life difficult since the professional adviser must constantly monitor the state trust accounting law in his or her jurisdiction to determine if any changes were made as well as the effective date of any changes.

The AICPA Task Force in an executive summary indicated, in essence, the following:

(1) Since the number and size of trusts and estates are growing, there is more of a need for competent fiduciary accounting services.

(2) Accountants who prepare fiduciary income tax returns must recognize that taxable income and fiduciary accounting income are not necessarily the same.

(3) Accountants must be aware of the difference between taxable income and fiduciary accounting income in order to avoid legal liability problems for trustees and beneficiaries.

(4) It is important for the accountant to read and understand the provisions in the trust document and/or will prior to preparing a fiduciary accounting.

(5) Accountants who are engaged to provide fiduciary accounting services have to know about the trust laws and trust codes that have been adopted in the state that governs the trust. In addition, state case law may affect the administration of the trust.

(6) The accountant should seek advice from competent counsel. Such counsel is an additional resource for the accountant.

Although the AICPA Task Force recommends that accountants develop an expertise in order to perform fiduciary accounting services, that suggestion is easier said than done.

The problem facing the accountant is that although fiduciary accounting services are important, the subject area is not an easy one to learn. The accountant who decides to offer these fiduciary accounting services must in essence become a subspecialist.

One way for the accountant to learn this area is by means of on-the-job training. The best way is to work with another accountant who is experienced in rendering fiduciary accounting services.

Another approach is to do extensive reading on the subject. However, there are only a few manuals addressing it.

I have found that there is a paucity of continued professional education programs that deal with fiduciary accounting rules under specific state trust laws. Most continuing education programs on fiduciary taxation focus on fiduciary tax return preparation and not on state-specific fiduciary accounting issues.

In addition, to my knowledge, graduate tax programs generally do not offer any course in fiduciary accounting that is state specific.

The Uniform Principal and Income Act of 1997 covers a number of subject areas, including

(1) definitions and fiduciary duties,
(2) the decedent's estate or terminating income interest,
(3) apportionment of beginning- and end-of-income interest,
(4) allocation of receipts during the administration of the trust, and
(5) allocation of disbursements during the administration of the trust.

WHAT YOU SHOULD KNOW ABOUT TRUSTS

Many individuals for various reasons have provided for trusts in their estate plans.

There are valid reasons for creating a trust:

- Asset protection
- Preventing the assets from being dissipated prematurely by heirs
- Providing that assets stay within the bloodline
- Providing an asset stream (income and/or principal) for heirs
- Providing for the health, education, maintenance, and support of heirs
- Providing for minors
- Providing a fund for payment of estate taxes, debts of the estate, and payment of administration expenses
- Providing for professional trustees who can invest the assets over the long term and who understand the trust laws
- Anticipating a will contest
- General difficulty of trust contests
- Avoiding ancillary probate proceedings if real property is located in multiple states (cost savings)
- Providing for the incapacity of the creator of the trust
- Privacy issues
- Federal and state estate tax savings
- Taking advantage of the expanded generation-skipping transfer tax exemptions

In the absence of specific reasons for a trust, there are many reasons why a long-term trust should not be provided for. These reasons include the following:

- Insufficient assets to warrant the establishment of a trust
- The accounting costs for maintaining records regarding trust transactions
- The annual tax reporting responsibilities of a trustee for preparing the fiduciary income tax return and the costs for such annual fiduciary income tax return preparation
- Preparation of annual accounting reports mandated by state trust laws in many states, including the costs of preparing such annual accounting reports
- The lack of a responsible trustee
- The potential liability of a trustee
- The complex state trust laws
- The lack of adequate professional advisers who are familiar with expanding litigation issues regarding trust issues
- The potential difficulty of obtaining releases from trust beneficiaries when the trust is closed out
- The need to do a trust accounting when a trustee dies, resigns, or becomes disabled in order to obtain releases from liability
- The need to maintain records for extended periods of time in order to avoid trustee liability
- Costs of trustee commissions over an extended period of time
- Costs of obtaining legal advice regarding trust issues
- Costs of defending trust litigation
- Requirements of giving information to the trust beneficiary
- Use of relatives and friends as trustees who are not technically competent
- Costs of having investment advisers
- Difficulty of keeping up with all the trust laws that are adopted by the particular jurisdiction
- Time demands on the trustee

It is important to note that the trust rules are complex and that trustees have significant obligations and potential liabilities. In view of the exploding amount of litigation against trustees, a trustee should generally be cautious before taking on a trustee appointment. Many trustees have regretted accepting the appointment since trust litigation against a trustee may extend over many years. Trust litigation today is big business. That is not to say that all trusts are the subject of trust litigation. Most trusts are not; however, a significant number are. Therefore, it is prudent for individuals to understand the trust rules, time demands, and potential liabilities they could face before they accept trustee positions.

There are many advantages in selecting an institutional trustee to administer a long-term trust:

- Experience in administering trusts
- Knowledge of the technical rules involving the interpretation of the trust laws in the jurisdiction
- Keeping up with the changes in the trust laws of the jurisdiction
- Responsibility for preparation of fiduciary income tax returns each year
- Responsibility for accountings to the trust beneficiaries
- Responsibility for investing trust assets consistent with the Prudent Investor Act
- Liability to the trust beneficiaries in the event the trustee commits a breach of trust
- Experience in investing trust assets
- Capitalization on investment management skills
- Maintenance of permanent records of trust assets for the life of the trust
- Elimination of liability of individual trustee(s) who are not competent
- Experience with the revised UPAIA rules that apply in most jurisdictions
- Experience with the UTC rules that apply in a number of jurisdictions
- Effective use of the power-of-adjustment rules that apply in most jurisdictions
- Knowledge of the applicable unitrust rules
- Impartiality in administering the trust
- Avoidance of possible conflicts that may occur if the trustee is an individual who has disagreements with the trust beneficiaries
- Information-reporting obligations to the trust beneficiaries

- Discouragement of litigation

The disadvantages of an institutional trustee include the following:

- Higher costs for trustee commissions
- Turnover of personnel in the trust department that is handling the trust relationship
- Psychological issues concerning the use of an institutional trustee

TRUSTEE LIABILITY ISSUES

Many individual trustees may not have access to accountants and/or attorneys who are skilled in fiduciary taxation and in fiduciary accounting services. In addition, accountants and/or attorneys who are skilled in fiduciary taxation and fiduciary accounting services are in high demand and generally command high hourly rates.

It is possible that annual fees for the preparation of annual fiduciary income tax returns may range from a low fee of several hundred dollars to an annual fee of several thousand dollars or more. The fees are based on many facts, including

(1) the number of transactions that the trust has during the calendar year,
(2) the time it takes the accountant to analyze the transactions, and
(3) determining the accounting income that must be paid to the trust beneficiaries.

The liability of the trustee may be triggered because the trustee does not engage a qualified accountant and/or trust attorney to assist him or her in understanding what the duties of a trustee entail.

If a trustee misinterprets the terms of the trust document, then he or she may have headaches if the trust beneficiary challenges the trustee's actions at a later date. This can happen if the trustee does not understand the terms of the trust document and does not retain a competent accountant or attorney to work with him or her.

Many individuals who act as a trustee may not be aware of the fact that the trust laws of the state that has jurisdiction of the trust have been completely revamped. These revised trust laws may catch a trustee off guard. It is possible that the trustee's ignorance, although innocent, may trigger significant liabilities against him or her at a later date.

It is extremely difficult for an individual trustee who does not have an adviser who is familiar with state-specific trust laws to have an awareness of all the potential issues that are involved in trust administration.

THE TAI TASK FORCE

According to the AICPA TAI Task Force, an individual who acts as a trustee needs to have a thorough understanding of the responsibilities of a trustee. There are many pressures that may be placed upon a trustee. The position is often a time-consuming task.

The TAI Task Force indicates in part what the basic responsibilities of a fiduciary are.

(1) *Obligation to manage trust assets.* This involves the obligation of the trustee to invest the trust assets in a prudent manner.

Author's Note

Most states have adopted some version of the Uniform Prudent Investor Act, which provides the rules that govern the actions of the trustee with respect to the investment of the trust assets.

If the trustee violates the Prudent Investor Act, then the trustee may have to explain his or her actions with respect to the investment performance to the trust beneficiaries. This is especially true when significant losses of trust assets take place. The Prudent Investor Act, of course, applies to a financial institution that acts as a trustee as well.

Even if the trustee follows the Prudent Investor Act, an unhappy trust beneficiary can always challenge the trustee's investment policy if the beneficiary is unhappy with the trust's investment performance.

A review should be made of the court decisions involving challenges to the trustee's actions regarding investment decisions in the state that has jurisdiction of the trust.

(2) *Obligation of loyalty.* The trustee has an obligation to act in the best interests of the trust and the trust beneficiaries. A trustee cannot directly and/or indirectly deal personally with the trust assets or make any personal profits as a result of his or her relationship with the trust.

15

Author's Note

If the trustee violates his or her obligation of loyalty to the trust or trust beneficiaries, then the trustee will be subject to sanctions by the court having jurisdiction of the trust in a trust accounting proceeding.

---

(3) *Obligation to account.* A few states have enacted versions of the UTC that have placed some type of obligation on the trustee to send an annual report to disclose certain financial information to certain trust beneficiaries. In those few states, the failure to satisfy this legal obligation can subject the trustee to sanctions by the court having jurisdiction over the trust. Most states that have adopted versions of the UTC for the most part avoid this legal obligation of the trustee to send annual disclosures to certain trust beneficiaries.

CONFLICTS OF INTEREST

Many accountants and attorneys often act as trustees. This may happen when the creator of the trust feels that he or she does not, for whatever reason, wish to select a family member or a financial institution as a trustee.

If an accountant or attorney is asked to serve as a trustee, then he or she should make sure that there are not any potential conflict-of-interest issues. Conflict-of-interest issues may be triggered for any number of reasons.

(1) The accountant or attorney who is considering serving as a trustee may also be performing professional services for one or more beneficiaries of the trust. If that situation is applicable, then the accountant or attorney should discuss this issue with all the appropriate parties and indicate that this is an issue that should be addressed before he or she is selected as a trustee.

(2) These professional services may involve advisory services, financial planning services, estate planning services, and tax return preparation services for the beneficiary of the trust.

(3) If the conflict-of-interest issue cannot be resolved, then the accountant or attorney should not agree to act as trustee.

Author's Note

The AICPA TAI Task Force discusses this conflict-of-interest issue in the *Practice Guide for Accountants Who Perform Fiduciary Accounting Services*.

The AICPA *Practice Guide* cautions accountants who may act as a trustee to be cautious and avoid any potential conflicts of interest. In the case of a potential conflict of interest, the accountant must feel that he or she can be objective in serving as trustee. The accountant, after full disclosure of the potential conflict of interest to the appropriate parties, should obtain written consents from such parties to the effect that they do not object to the accountant's serving as trustee. However, the trustee remaindermen who are not parties to these written consents may still challenge the trustee decades later.

* * *

Author's Note

A potential conflict of interest for the accountant who acts as a trustee may exist, for example, in the following situations:

1. The accountant, as a trustee under the terms of the trust, has the discretion to pay income to a trust beneficiary or accumulate income. The accountant also performs professional services for the trust beneficiary. In the event that the trustee pays income to the trust beneficiary, the trust remainderman can accuse the accountant of not acting in an impartial manner and/or favoring the discretionary trust income beneficiary in a court accounting proceeding.

2. The accountant, as a trustee under the terms of the trust, is required to pay the trust income each year to the trust income beneficiary. In addition, under the terms of the trust, the accountant, as a trustee, has the broad discretion to invade principal on behalf of the trust income beneficiary for the comfort of the trust income beneficiary. The accountant also performs professional services for the trust income beneficiary. In the event that the trustee invades principal for the trust income beneficiary, then the trust remainderman can accuse the accountant of not acting in an impartial manner and/or favoring the trust income beneficiary in a court accounting proceeding commenced by the trust remainderman.

3. The accountant, as a trustee, is required to pay the trust income each year to the trust income beneficiary. In addition, the accountant, as a trustee, also performs professional services for the trust remainderman. The trustee has no power to invade principal on behalf of the trust income beneficiary. During the calendar year 2014, the trust income amounts to 1 percent of the average value of the trust assets. The accountant, as the trustee, fails to exercise the power to adjust the trust income to a greater percentage even though permitted to do so under the state trust law. This power to adjust is provided for under the state trust law in many states. The trust income beneficiary can accuse the accountant, as a trustee, of not acting in an impartial manner and/or favoring the trust remainderman in a court accounting proceeding that is commenced by the trust income beneficiary.

* * *

Author's Note

The comments described above regarding the accountant's acting as a trustee and the conflict-of-interest issues may apply to an attorney who acts as a trustee and who also performs professional services for a trust beneficiary.

Under these circumstances, the attorney is in an extremely difficult position. In my opinion, the attorney, before accepting the appointment as a trustee, should advise the appropriate parties that the attorney feels that he or she can act in an objective manner. In addition, the attorney should consider obtaining written consent from the appropriate parties that they do not object to the attorney's serving as trustee. Once again, such written consent does not preclude a challenge by the trust remainderman at a later date.

Author's Note

The AICPA *Practice Guide* cautions the accountant that acting as a trustee can be a time-consuming responsibility.

Although the accountant who may be selected as a trustee is generally a qualified individual, he or she should recognize the time constraints and fiduciary duties that are being taken on.

Accountants tend to be worthwhile candidates for the appointment as trustee for many reasons. For the most part, they are used to working under time constraints and have organizational skills and the ability to maintain the records that are necessary in order to render fiduciary accounting services.

As long as the accountant is willing to take on the responsibilities of a trustee and can avoid the potential conflict-of-interest issues, then he or she should consider taking on the assignment.

However, the accountant should recognize that the trustee must be willing to keep on top of the trust accounting income and principal rules under the state trust laws; the statutory annual reporting requirements, if any, under the state trust laws; and significant case law developments in the state.

The accountant who acts as a trustee must understand the provisions of the trust documents. In the event that he or she does not understand any of the provisions, then he or she should have the trust document explained by trust counsel.

In my opinion, the accountant who acts as a trustee should request that trust counsel explain the state trust laws. In addition, the accountant who acts as a trustee should obtain copies of the appropriate statutes under the state trust laws that apply to the trust and become familiar with these laws. These state trust laws may include the following:

(1) the Uniform Principal and Income Act (UPAIA) applicable to the state,

(2) the Prudent Investor Act applicable to the state, and

(3) the Uniform Trust Code (UTC) applicable to the state. The Prudent Investor Act provisions are often included in the UTC.

The District of Columbia is included whenever the term *state* is used.

It is also important to recognize that state trust laws are revised from time to time. For example, although many states currently have a UTC, many do not. However, there is currently a trend toward the adoption of a version of the UTC in a number of additional states.

In addition, most states have adopted versions of the 1997 UPAIA. Amendments are also adopted by many states from time to time with various effective dates.

The trustee must be aware of not only the changing state trust laws but also the significant court cases in the state that interpret the state trust laws. In addition, the state trust laws may be changed from time to time as a result of technical corrections to the state trust law and for other reasons.

Once again, the accountant, as a trustee, must recognize that trust administration is a responsibility that must not be taken lightly. This is especially true today because of the expanding liability exposure that a trustee has in litigation.

One wonders how a friend or family member who takes on a trustee appointment would react if the details about what is involved in acting as a trustee were explained in advance. I am sure that only the most dedicated individual would venture into the land of acting as a trustee if the pitfalls and responsibilities were made clear.

Before an individual creates a trust, he or she should be informed on how a trust works. This discussion should include the following points.

(1) The reasons why a trust may be important in his or her family situation:

    a.   If the trust beneficiary is not able to handle funds or if the trust beneficiary has creditor rights issues, then the trust may be worthwhile.

    b.   The creator of the trust for the benefit of a child may desire that the remaindermen of the trust assets be the grandchildren.

    c.   The creator of the trust may wish to provide a nest egg for the grandchildren.

    d.   The creator of the trust may wish to have the trust assets stay within the bloodline.

    e.   The creator of the trust may wish to save federal and state estate taxes and do his or her estate planning by means of the use of a trust.

    f.   The creator of the trust may wish to take advantage of the expanded generation-skipping transfer tax exemption.

    g.   The creator of a trust may wish to establish an irrevocable life insurance trust for estate tax purposes and for other reasons.

    h.   The creator of the trust may wish to provide for a disabled or incompetent member of the family.

    i.   The creator of the trust may expect a will contest. If the assets are already in a revocable or irrevocable trust at the time of his or her death, then it will be more difficult to set aside a trust in litigation.

    j.   Probate filing fees in a specific state may be reduced if assets are in a revocable trust as of the date of the trust creator's death.

    k.   If the creator of the trust is not well or has difficulty functioning, then having the assets in a trust may be worthwhile.

(2) The creator of the trust should be aware of the costs of administering a trust. After death, these are continuing costs that are involved in maintaining and administering a trust. These costs may include:

    a.   Annual trustee commissions

    b.   Annual accounting fees for the preparation of fiduciary income tax returns

    c.   Investment advisory fees

    d.   Annual accounting fees for the preparation of annual reports to trust beneficiaries, if applicable

    e.   Costs for preparing periodic or final accountings that need to be filed with the court in order for the trustee to be released from liability. This requirement is based on the requirements of the state that has jurisdiction of the trust.

(3) If a trustee is disabled, then an interim accounting may be necessary in order for the disabled trustee to be released from liability.

(4) If a trustee dies, then an interim accounting may be necessary in order for the trustee's estate to be released from liability.

(5) It is important to consider fees paid to trust counsel to update the trust, to the extent possible, with regard to changes in the trust laws in the state that has jurisdiction of the trust.

Author's Note

If the amount of potential trust assets are not significant, then tread softly before you consider a trust. The costs of running a trust for decades may run into the tens of thousands of dollars or more, depending on the amount of potential fees involved in administering the trust. In addition, the complexities of the terms of the trust and the changes in state trust laws that may take place from time to time may result in increased professional fees as well.

Many individuals create trusts for valid reasons. Others create trusts because of such reasons as avoiding probate. If it makes sense for economic or other reasons, then use a trust. However, for example, if avoiding probate saves probate costs of $1,250, but the estimated cost of administering a trust for 20 years is $20,000 in accounting fees and trustee commissions, then the arrangement does not make economic sense. Evaluate the need for the trust when the potential assets in the trust are modest.

WHAT'S THE BIG DEAL ABOUT TRUSTS AND TRUST ADMINISTRATION?

In the last decade or so, there has been a movement toward unifying state trust laws. The movement is based in part on the extraordinary efforts of the National Conference of Commissioners on Uniform State Laws (NCCUSL). As a result of the efforts of the NCCUSL, the UPAIA was drafted in 1997 and further amended thereafter.

The purpose of the comprehensive draft was to provide the states with a model so that each state could decide whether or not to adopt the suggested recommendations of the NCCUSL as part of the state's own revised trust law.

Many states have adopted versions of the UPAIA in whole or in part. When a state adopts a version of the UPAIA, it also selects an effective date.

The UPAIA has a significant impact on how accounting income is to be determined by the trustee. Many fiduciary accounting rules are provided for under the UPAIA. Some of the accounting rules are discretionary in nature and others are mandatory.

If a trust provides that the income beneficiary must receive income each year, then legal problems may develop if the trustee does not know about the UPAIA provisions that apply to the trust. When a trustee must pay out income to a trust beneficiary, then he or she must determine the amount of income in a state that has adopted the UPAIA according to the provisions of the UPAIA that apply to that state. Income under state trust law and income under the Internal Revenue Code are not generally determined in the same manner. The trustee, in order to protect himself or herself, should ask trust counsel for advice about the UPAIA provisions that apply to the trust in the particular jurisdiction as well as any other trust accounting rules that apply.

If a trust provides that the income beneficiary may receive income each year in the discretion of the trustee, then the trustee, before exercising that discretion, should know how to determine the trust's fiduciary accounting income. This is necessary so that the trustee does not erroneously overpay the income beneficiary in the event the trustee exercises his or her discretion.

Certain trust accounting rules may be found in other provisions of the state trust laws as well. For example, in the New York State version of the UPAIA, nothing is stated about what portion of trustee commissions is charged against income or principal. That rule is found in another part of the state trust law.

In the model version of the UPAIA, one-half of the regular compensation of the trustee is charged to income and one-half is charged to principal. A number of states that have adopted a version of the UPAIA may not follow this rule.

Again, the point is that a state is not obligated to adopt the UPAIA. Over 40 states have adopted versions of the model UPAIA with various effective dates.

Therefore, each trustee is responsible for administering the trust based on the provisions of the trust document and the state trust laws.

As a practical matter, an individual who acts as a trustee without knowing the rules acts at his or her own peril.

Unfortunately, many individuals do not realize the potential liability that they face. If the trustee is challenged on technical issues, then he or she may have difficulty in defending his or her actions.

The bottom line is that an individual trustee must have the rules explained to him or her by someone who knows the trust rules and should not go merrily on his or her way. In the real world, when the trust assets are not significant and the trustee makes innocent mistakes that do not result in a financial detriment of any substance to the beneficiaries, then the trustee may not have a problem. This, of course, assumes that the trustee and the trust beneficiaries get along.

Author's Note

When a trust document refers to income, then income is determined under the trust accounting rules of the state trust law. In addition, when a trust refers to principal, then principal is determined under the state trust law. Income determined under the Internal Revenue Code and income determined under the state trust law are for the most part not determined in the same manner.

WHY TRUSTS ARE DIFFICULT TO ADMINISTER

Trusts are often long-winded instruments that are difficult for the average individual trustee (who is not a professional) to understand. In addition, if the trustee does not retain an accountant or an attorney who is aware of the state trust laws, then the trustee may have a problem in administering the trust.

Not only must a trustee read the trust instrument, he or she must understand the document and follow its terms. If the trust instrument provides that income must be paid out annually to the income beneficiary, then the trustee must determine the amount of income that must be paid out each year.

If a trustee may, at his or her discretion, pay out income each year to a trust income beneficiary, then the trustee must exercise discretion in good faith. In addition, the trustee must look to the terms of the trust instrument for guidance in exercising the discretion that is granted to him or her.

Ultimately, the trustee must account for his or her actions with respect to handling the affairs of the trust. Not only is the trustee responsible for the proper handling of the investments of the trust assets, but he or she is responsible for following the terms of the trust regarding distributions to the income beneficiary of the trust.

In addition, the trustee may be granted discretion regarding the invasion of principal for the benefit of the current trust income beneficiary. Once again, a good faith requirement is imposed on the trustee.

The task of acting as a trustee is not a cakewalk. It is more often than not a headache for the nonprofessional trustee, since it is both time consuming and subject, in many cases, to modest trustee commissions.

Often, members of the family act as trustee without compensation. This is a labor of love, not money.

Since many trusts last for decades, the trustee should realize that the responsibility is often long term, and though it may be initially rewarding, down the road it will be a difficult and ongoing assignment.

During the operation of the trust, the trustee may have to periodically account to the trust beneficiaries. At the end of the trust, when the trust assets are to be distributed to the ultimate trust beneficiaries, the trustee will have to account for the operations of the trust as well. An accounting to the ultimate trust beneficiaries may be both expensive and time consuming. It may span a period of many decades. It is important that the trust records be maintained in case the trustee is challenged for his or her actions. Obviously, if the trustee dies, becomes incompetent, or loses the trust records, then problems may be triggered by trust beneficiaries who are unhappy with the trustee's actions during the period of his or her administration of the trust.

When everyone gets along, then it may not be that big of a headache, but if a trust beneficiary does not like the trustee for whatever reason, then problems may arise.

Trusts are big business, and many law firms and financial planners recommend the use of trusts from an asset-protection point of view.

When the stakes are high, it is best that an institutional trustee be considered. Even though the fees of an institutional trustee are greater than those of a nonprofessional trustee, it may be a good move in the long run.

Obviously, an institutional trustee can handle a trust that lasts for decades without running into the problem of death or disability that would apply to an individual trustee.

An institutional trustee has deep pockets, so it has the ability to defend itself and pay for any damages that may occur during the administration of the trust.

MULTIPLE TRUSTEES

If the grantor of a trust selects two trustees to administer a trust, then problems may arise if the trustees do not get along. Obviously, if there are three trustees, then they may act for the most part by majority decisions.

A grantor may select multiple trustees to take advantage of the knowledge and thought processes of more than one mind. In addition, if two or more individuals are serving as trustees, then there is theoretically more of a safety factor regarding the protection of the trust assets.

In the case involving multiple trustees, the trustees must be on the ball. A trustee who merrily goes along with the actions of the other trustee(s) is potentially on the hook if trust assets are administered improperly.

If a cotrustee does not agree with the actions of the other trustee(s), then he or she must take appropriate action to prevent any improper acts. State law will determine what action the cotrustee must take if he or she does not agree with the position taken by the majority of trustees.

Many states have adopted a version of the UTC. For example, the Maine version of the UTC is called the Maine Uniform Trust Code.

Section 703 of the Maine version of the UTC provides, in essence, that a trustee who does not join in the action of another trustee may not be liable for the action of the other trustee unless a serious breach of trust is involved; then the dissenting trustee must take action to prevent a cotrustee from committing a serious violation. If a serious violation has occurred, action must be taken by the dissenting trustee to correct the breach of trust by the cotrustee.

Obviously, the dissenting trustee should always notify the cotrustee(s) of his or her objections in writing before the action is taken, in order to document his or her position. If the infraction is not significant, then the dissenting trustee is not liable, provided that he or she has documented the dissent. Always remember that a passive trustee may have significant liability if he or she goes along with a cotrustee who acts improperly.

It may be worthwhile to have an institutional trustee serve together with a family member trustee. This is important because the family member trustee will have a personal relationship with the trust beneficiaries. In addition, the institutional trustee should have the technical skills that are necessary in interpreting the trust document and the technical knowledge that is necessary in order to interpret the state trust laws.

The combination of an institutional trustee and a family member trustee is important from a continuity point of view as well. This continuity issue is important since a trust can span decades. The individual trustee may not wish to spend a lifetime administering a trust. The institutional trustee theoretically has a perpetual life.

In addition, a trust beneficiary will think twice before commencing a contest against an institutional trustee.

The only disadvantage of having an institutional trustee working with a family member trustee is the additional cost of trustee commissions that the institutional trustee will receive. An institutional trustee generally charges a higher trustee commission than a family member trustee. However, the institutional trustee can bring to the table a great deal of technical knowledge. In addition, the institutional trustee may provide a comfort level to the family member trustee who, as he or she ages, becomes concerned about death or disability. Further, an institutional trustee generally has greater record-retention capability.

RIGHTS OF TRUSTEES TO COMPENSATION

A trustee has a right to be compensated and to receive reasonable compensation. If there are multiple trustees, then depending on state trust law, there may be multiple trustee commissions. A state trust law could allow compensation to be determined based on percentages of trust assets. New York State trust laws provide for annual trustee commissions to be paid based on percentages of trust assets. It is possible, under New York State law, to provide for the specific compensation for a trustee.

Many state trust laws provide that if the terms of the trust document do not provide for specific compensation of a trustee, then the trustee is entitled to receive reasonable compensation. Counsel for the trust should advise the potential trustee with respect to the manner of determining reasonable compensation in a given jurisdiction.

RIGHT OF TRUSTEE TO REIMBURSEMENT OF EXPENSES

A trustee who personally advances funds on behalf of the trust for proper expenses is entitled to be reimbursed from the trust funds.

In the event that the trustee personally advances funds for legal fees and costs in connection with a breach of trust proceeding against him or her, such expenses may or may not be reimbursed from the trust fund. If the trustee loses, then he or she should not be reimbursed. If the trustee wins, then he or she is reimbursed to the extent these expenses are reasonable.

REMEDIES FOR
BREACH OF TRUST

A breach of trust takes place when a trustee violates a duty that he or she owes to a beneficiary.

The UTC provides for remedies that a beneficiary can seek against the trustee.

Section 1001 of the Maine Uniform Trust Code provides in part as follows:

Remedies for breach of trust:

1. *Violation of Duty.* A violation by a trustee of a duty the trustee owes to a beneficiary is a breach of trust.

2. *Remedies.* To remedy a breach of trust that has occurred or may occur, the court may:

1. Compel the trustee to perform the trustee's duties;

2. Enjoin the trustee from continuing a breach of trust;

3. Compel the trustee to redress a breach of trust by paying money, restoring the property or other means;

4. Order a trustee to account;

5. Appoint a special fiduciary to take possession of the trust property and administer the trust;

6. Suspend the trustee;

7. Remove the trustee;

8. Reduce or deny compensation to the trustee;

9. . . . Void an act of the trustee; impose a lien or a constructive trust on trust property, or trace property wrongfully disposed of and recover the property or its proceeds; or

10. Order any other appropriate relief.

Author's Note

If a successor trustee is appointed, he or she may commence a proceeding against the prior trustee in the event that the prior trustee has committed a breach of trust. Prior to accepting the appointment as a successor trustee, the potential successor trustee should examine the actions of the prior trustee in order to know what he or she may be getting into. If it looks like a big headache, then the potential successor trustee may not wish to accept the appointment.

Author's Note

If a state has not adopted a version of the UTC, then the beneficiary may use the remedies for breach of trust that are otherwise applicable to the state that has jurisdiction of the trust.

STATUTE OF LIMITATIONS

The statute of limitations in commencing a proceeding against a trustee may be a real headache for a trustee. It depends on the laws of the state that has jurisdiction over the trust. Each state has different rules. For example, the statute of limitations rules in New York and in Florida are completely different.

According to the UTC, the failure of the trustee to give a beneficiary an adequate report that meets certain guidelines may present a statute-of-limitations problem for the trustee. However, many states that have adopted versions of the UTC do not mandate annual disclosures to a trust beneficiary or the representative of a trust beneficiary.

Section 1005 of the Maine Uniform Trust Code provides in part as follows:

Limitation of action against trustee

(1) *Report; one-year limitation.* A beneficiary may not commence a proceeding against a trustee for breach of trust more than one year after the date the beneficiary or a representative of the beneficiary was sent a report that adequately disclosed the existence of a potential claim for breach of trust and informed the beneficiary of the time allowed for commencing a proceeding.

(2) *Disclosure of potential claim.* A report adequately discloses the existence of a potential claim for breach of trust if it provides sufficient information so that the beneficiary or representative knows of the potential claim or should have inquired into its existence.

(3) *Six years.* If subsection 1 does not apply, a judicial proceeding by a beneficiary against a trustee for breach of trust must be commenced within six years after the first to occur of:

1. The removal, resignation, or death of the trustee;
2. The termination of the beneficiary's interest in the trust; and

3. The termination of the trust.

Author's Note

The one-year statute of limitations starts only if the report is sent and also informs the beneficiaries or their representatives in some manner about a potential claim against the trustee and about the one-year statute of limitations for commencing a proceeding against the trustee.

In the event that the trustee does not send a report to the appropriate beneficiaries or their representatives that informs them about a possible claim against the trustee and the one-year period to commence proceeding, then the six-year statute-of-limitations period for beneficiaries to commence a proceeding against the trustee is applicable.

The statute of limitations rules in states that have adopted versions of the UTC are not generally the same. In addition, states that have not adopted a version of the UTC generally have different statute-of-limitations rules as well.

A potential trustee who is considering the appointment should ask the trust attorney about the statute of limitations that applies to trustees serving in a particular jurisdiction. For example, trusts subject to the jurisdiction of New York State for the most part do not have any statute of limitations with respect to proceedings against trustees.

ESTATE TAX ISSUES

A trustee who is also a trustee for a beneficiary should be precluded in the trust document from making a discretionary distribution to himself or herself for any arbitrary reason. State law may automatically provide for this rule and must be checked. However, if the trustee may, according to the trust document, make a discretionary distribution to himself or herself only for his or her health, education, maintenance, and support, then that provision should work as long as it does not conflict with state law. The purpose behind this provision is primarily related to estate taxes. It prevents the trust assets from being included in determining the estate tax liability of the trustee upon the trustee's subsequent death.

In addition, the trust document should provide that the trustee may not exercise a power to make any discretionary distribution of any kind (whether limited to a standard or otherwise) to a trust beneficiary to satisfy a legal support obligation that the trustee has to the trust beneficiary. This provision is necessary if the trustee is, for example, the trustee for his or her minor children and dies with this discretionary power. State law may automatically provide for this rule and must be checked.

Example: A number of states have adopted a version of the UTC, including Maine. The Maine Uniform Trust Code provides in part that "a trustee may not exercise a power to make discretionary distributions to satisfy a legal obligation of support that the trustee owes another person."

Caution: Just because state X has automatic protective provisions in the law does not mean that your state has such automatic protective language.

FIDUCIARY INCOME TAX RETURNS

A trust is a separate legal entity and is generally treated as such for accounting, legal, and tax purposes.

One should bear in mind that after the trust is funded, generally annual fiduciary income tax returns must be filed with the IRS and with the state (if applicable). There are certain exceptions to the annual filing requirements where the creator of the trust (grantor) is considered to be the owner of the trust for income tax purposes.

The preparation of the annual federal fiduciary income tax return (Form 1041) may be a simple or difficult assignment, depending on many factors. These factors include

(1) the terms of the trust document and
(2) the state trust laws governing the trust document.

Under the Internal Revenue Code, a trust can be a simple trust or a complex trust.

Basically, a simple trust under the IRS rules requires the trustee to distribute the trust income annually to the income beneficiary or beneficiaries, as the case may be.

A simple trust does not necessarily mean that the preparation of the trust income tax return is an inexpensive proposition. The accountant who prepares the fiduciary federal income tax return must first read the trust document and understand it. Obviously, the trustee who may be a family member or a friend has the ultimate responsibility of reading and understanding the terms of the trust document.

If the trustee has difficulty in determining the meaning of the terms of the document, then he or she should ask for help.

If, for example, Jack's trust document states that after his death, his son, Joseph, shall receive all of the income from the trust annually, then the trust is considered a simple trust since Joseph must receive the trust income each year.

But that's not the end of the story. Income under state trust laws and income under the Internal Revenue Code are often different amounts.

The IRS instructions for Form 1041 state, in part, as follows:

> Before preparing Form 1041, the fiduciary must figure the account-ing income of the . . . trust under the will or trust instrument and applicable local law to determine the amount, if any, of income that is required to be distributed, because the income distribution deduc-tion is based, in part, on that amount.

It is interesting to note that in a simple trust, the accounting income must be paid to Joseph. However, under state law, a capital gain is not for the most part considered to be accounting income but is instead considered to be principal.

EXAMPLE

If Jack died in 2013 and the trust received $25,000 in taxable interest income and dividends and had accounting fees and other deductible expenses of $2,000, all of which are charged against income under the state trust law, then Joseph would receive $23,000 from the trust for the calendar year 2013.

That amount is the trust accounting income for the calendar year 2013. This example assumes that all deductible expenses are charged against income under the UPAIA. Under the UPAIA and state trust laws, certain deductible expenses are allocated between income and principal. State laws must be checked.

In a simple trust, Joseph is taxed on the $23,000 amount on his per-sonal income tax return Form 1040 for the calendar year 2013, even if he actually receives the money in 2014 or at a later date. In addition, the trustee may allocate the expenses of $2,000 to either the taxable interest income or to dividend income in any manner that the trustee wishes. The trust is not taxed based on these facts.

Let's change the facts in the preceding example. Assume that the trust had a short-term capital gain of $4,000 for the calendar year 2013 in addition to the taxable interest income and dividend income. Also assume that the accounting fees and other deductible expenses amount to $2,000. In that case, the accounting income that Joseph must receive for the calendar year 2013 is still $23,000. The short-term capital gain of $4,000 is generally considered principal and is reported as a short-term capital gain on the trust return (Form 1041) for the calendar year 2013. The trust is taxed on the $4,000 short-term capital gain for the calendar year 2013.

Obviously, the trustee must be aware of the fact that a capital gain is not considered to be trust accounting income under state trust law unless the trust document provides otherwise.

The examples described above are rather straightforward. However, over 40 states have changed their state trust laws in recent years to permit an independent trustee to exercise certain powers. One of these powers is called the "power to adjust." This power may be exercised by the trustee if he or she invests primarily in equities and the accounting income of the trust (interest income and dividend income) is inadequate. For example, Harry's trust assets held in a simple trust amount to $1 million as of January 2, 2014. Also assume that for the calendar year 2014, the trust is estimated to earn approximately $10,000 in taxable interest income and dividend income. In addition, for the calendar year 2014, the equities are expected to earn approximately 6 percent. Both estimates are made in November 2014. In such a case, the independent trustee has the power to increase the distribution to the income beneficiary by a reasonable amount by means of exercising the power to adjust. The trustee in his or her discretion exercises the power of adjustment before the end of 2014 according to the state trust law in most jurisdictions. This can be done by a journal entry actually dated by the trustee prior to the end of 2014. So, the trustee can, for example, determine to transfer an additional $20,000 from principal to income for the calendar year 2014. This $20,000 amount is income tax–free to the trust beneficiary. A power to adjust is basically the ability of a trustee to transfer principal to income or income to principal pursuant to certain guidelines under the state trust law in over 40 states.

According to the state law in over 40 states, the trustee may consider a number of factors in the state law, as discussed, in order to determine whether to exercise the power to adjust.

In general, the trustee may exercise a power to adjust in an impartial manner that is fair and reasonable to all of the beneficiaries (income beneficiaries and remaindermen). The state law indicates the factors that the trustee, to the extent relevant, should look at.

Let's assume that the trust beneficiary of Harry's trust is his son, Jack. Jack is the income beneficiary of Harry's trust, and the trust states that Jack shall receive the income from the trust each year. Mark is an independent trustee of Harry's trust. The taxable income of the trust for 2014 is estimated to be approximately $10,000 after expenses. The trust does not provide for the invasion of principal by Mark, trustee on behalf of Jack. If Mark decides prior to December 31, 2014, to exercise the power to adjust in favor of Jack to the extent of $20,000, then Jack is entitled to receive $30,000 from Harry's trust for the calendar year 2014. Although the accounting income of the trust now becomes $30,000 under the power-to-adjust rules, Jack is taxed on only $10,000 (the taxable income of the trust). In essence, Jack receives the extra $20,000 income tax–free. Principal is converted to accounting income, not taxable income.

The point of the example is that trust accounting income and taxable income are not the same amount. The IRS has issued final regulations and states that the power-to-adjust rule is acceptable for IRS purposes if it is permitted under the state trust law.

A complex trust exists under the IRS rules whenever a trustee distributes principal from a trust to a trust beneficiary. The trust document would have to authorize the trustee to invade principal on behalf of a trust beneficiary on some basis. For example, a trustee distributes or is required to distribute the trust income to the beneficiary but, in addition, invades principal pursuant to the terms of the trust and pays that principal amount to the trust income beneficiary. In that case, the trust is considered a complex trust. In general, a distribution of principal to a trust beneficiary is a nontaxable distribution as well.

Author's Note

The trust adviser must become familiar with the power-to-adjust and UPAIA rules that apply in the state that has jurisdiction of the trust. If the trust adviser doesn't know how the rules work, then the trustee can have headaches. The nonprofessional trustee would not generally know about the rules unless informed by the trust adviser. The trustee may have to defend his or her actions, and ignorance of the law is generally not a good defense. The institutional trustees are familiar with the trust accounting rules in the state that has jurisdiction of the trust.

As a final note, there are very few continuing education programs that are conducted for attorneys or certified public accountants that cover the subject of the trust accounting income and principal rules on an in-depth basis that are state specific.

UNITRUST

A number of states have provisions that involve unitrust provisions under the state trust law. These provisions may be incorporated in a state's version of the UPAIA or be in a separate statute.

The rules involved in a unitrust provision are technical in nature. Over 20 states have unitrust provisions.

Basically, a unitrust provision generally permits the trustee to determine the accounting income of the trust based on a fixed percentage of the net fair market value of the trust's assets held in the trust as of the beginning of the trust's valuation year.

For example, assume that Carl is a mandatory income beneficiary of Martin's trust. At the beginning of the trust's accounting year 2014, the trust assets are valued at $1 million. The trustee has elected that the unitrust provisions apply to Martin's trust. The unitrust percentage that applies to Martin's trust in state is 4 percent. In essence, Carl must receive $40,000 ($1 million × 4 percent = $40,000) from Martin's trust for the calendar year 2014 as accounting income, regardless of the actual earnings of the trust.

If, for example, Martin's trust has only $10,000 of net earnings for the calendar year 2014, Carl still receives $40,000. In a unitrust, the amount of $40,000 that Carl must receive is not reduced by any expenses. Also, Carl is taxed only on the net taxable earnings of the trust. If the $10,000 of net earnings of the trust is made up of taxable interest income, then Carl is taxed on only $10,000, and the difference between the $40,000 that he receives and the $10,000 that he is taxed on is a tax-free distribution. In this case, Carl receives a tax-free distribution of $30,000.

The IRS has issued final regulations and states that the unitrust concept is acceptable for IRS purposes if it is permitted under the state trust law.

ESTATE PLANNING AND PROFESSIONAL LIABILITY

A case of first impression that was decided by the Court of Appeals of New York on June 17, 2010, involved the ability of the personal representative of an estate to maintain a legal malpractice claim against an attorney.

The court's opinion was significant since it held that the personal representative of the estate had standing to sue an attorney.

Prior to the June 17, 2010, opinion in the *Estate of Schneider* case (2010 NY Slip Op 05281), the New York courts have held that a third party without privity could not maintain a malpractice claim against an attorney "absent fraud, collusion, malicious acts or other special circumstances" (see *Spivey v. Pulley*, 138 AD2d 563, 564 [2d Dept 1988]). However, the Court of Appeals in the *Schneider* case reversed prior case law in New York and held in part as follows:

> We now hold that privity, or a relationship sufficiently approaching privity, exists between the personal representative of an estate and the estate planning attorney. We agree with the Texas Supreme Court that the estate "stands in the shoes of a Decedent" and therefore "has the capacity to maintain the malpractice claim on the estate's behalf" (Belt v Oppenheimer, Blend, Harrison & Tate, Inc. 192 SW3d 780 [Tex 2006]. The personal representative of an estate should not be prevented from raising a negligent estate planning claim against the attorney who caused harm to the estate. The attorney estate planner surely knows that minimizing the tax burden of the estate is one of the central tasks entrusted to the professional.

Thus, based on the *Schneider* case, the estate has a right to maintain an action for a legal malpractice claim against an estate planning attorney.

The case does not stand for the proposition that legal malpractice was committed by the attorney but merely lets the case go forward to determine whether or not there was a valid legal malpractice claim against the attorney.

The issue of first impression before the Court of Appeals was:

> whether an attorney may be held liable for damages resulting from negligent representation in estate tax planning that causes enhanced estate tax liability. We hold that a personal representative of an estate may maintain a legal malpractice claim for such pecuniary losses to the estate.

According to the opinion, the estate's complaint against the estate planning attorney alleges the following facts:

> Defendants represented decedent Saul Schneider from at least April 2000 to his death in October 2006. In April 2000, decedent purchased a $1 million life insurance policy. Over several years, he transferred ownership of that property from himself to an entity of which he was principal owner, then to another entity of which he was principal owner and then, in 2005, back to himself. At his death in October 2006, the proceeds of the insurance policy were included as part of his gross taxable estate. Decedent's estate commenced this malpractice action in 2007, alleging that defendants negligently advised decedent to transfer, or failed to advise decedent not to transfer, the policy which resulted in an increased estate tax liability.

The opinion in *Schneider* referred in a footnote to EPTL 11-3.2(b) that provides in part as follows:

> Action by personal representative for injury to person or property. No cause of action for injury to person or property is lost because of the death of the person in whose favor the cause of action existed. For any injury an action may be brought or continued by the personal representative of the decedent.

The opinion also states in part as follows:

> Despite the holding in this case, strict priority remains a bar against beneficiaries and other third-party individuals' estate planning malpractice claims absent fraud or other circumstances.

Executive Summary

(1) The case permits the legal representative of the estate to pursue a claim of estate planning malpractice against the attorney.

(2) The case does not decide whether or not estate planning malpractice by the attorney did in fact take place.

Caution: Although the *Schneider* case involved an estate planning attorney, there is the potential for the points mentioned in this case to be expanded to include nonattorney estate planners and/or financial planners who hold themselves out to be estate planners.

LIFE INSURANCE AND ESTATE TAX ISSUES

Many individuals in the United States own life insurance policies. In the event that an individual dies and owns a life insurance policy, then for estate tax purposes the proceeds of the life insurance policy are included in his or her gross estate.

If the surviving spouse is the beneficiary, then the proceeds of the life insurance policy are not subject to an estate tax since the proceeds qualify as a marital deduction. However, if the life insurance proceeds are payable to other than the surviving spouse or a qualifying charity, then they can be subject to a federal estate tax and/or a state estate tax.

Since the federal estate tax exemption as of the calendar year 2013 is $5,250,000 and subject to inflation adjustments, then an individual who dies with less than the threshold amount should not be concerned about whether his or her estate will be subject to a federal estate tax liability. The life insurance proceeds are included in determining whether or not the threshold amount is satisfied. Also, adjusted taxable gifts are included in determining whether or not the threshold amount is satisfied. In 2014, the threshold amount for the federal estate tax exemption increased to $5,340,000.

Even if the threshold amount for federal estate tax is high, the state estate tax or state inheritance tax exemption can be a lot lower.

Many states have estate tax exemptions that are considerably less than the federal estate tax exemption. A number of states do not have any state estate taxes. In those states that have state estate taxes, the tax rate can be significant.

An example based on hypothetical State X law follows:

Harry, the taxpayer, is single and has a taxable estate is State X (excluding any life insurance policies) of $1,000,000. Assume that State X's exemption for state estate tax liability is $1,000,000.

The beneficiary of his estate is Carl, his nephew. If Harry dies in the calendar year 2014, then the federal estate tax liability is zero and the State X estate tax liability is zero. This assumes that Harry has not made any taxable gifts above the annual exclusion amount during his lifetime.

Now let's change the example and add that Harry also owns a term-life insurance policy of $1,000,000 on his life. The beneficiary of his life insurance policy is Carl.

If Harry dies in the calendar year 2014, then the taxable estate is now $2,000,000 instead of $1,000,000. Assume that the estate tax rate in State X on the $1,000,000 in excess of the State X exemption amount is 7 percent. The federal estate tax is still zero because Harry's estate is under the federal threshold amount of $5,340,000. However, the State X estate tax liability on a $2,000,000 taxable estate is now $70,000.

Under the State X law, the life insurance policy is included in Harry's taxable estate for State X estate tax purposes. Other states may or may not include life insurance proceeds for purposes of determining state estate taxes or state inheritance taxes. Counsel should research this. However, for federal estate tax purposes, the life insurance policy owned by Harry is in the count.

In order to avoid the $70,000 State X estate tax liability, the policy should have been owned by an irrevocable trust or by Carl directly and not by Harry.

If Harry is made aware of this issue, then he could transfer the ownership of the life insurance policy during his lifetime to Carl or to an irrevocable trust for the benefit of Carl and hope that he lives more than three years after the date of the transfer. In the event that he dies during the three-year period, then the life insurance policy is still included in the count for estate tax purposes.

The three-year rule can be avoided if Carl owned and was the beneficiary of the life insurance policy from inception or if an irrevocable trust was initially created and owned the life insurance policy for the benefit of Carl.

Author's Note

Life insurance policies owned by a retirement plan are included in the gross estate of the plan participant on his or her death. It may or may not be worthwhile to have a life insurance feature in a retirement plan if it triggers significant additional federal and/or state estate tax liabilities. Counsel should review this issue with the plan participant.

IRREVOCABLE LIFE INSURANCE TRUSTS AND ESTATE PLANNING

Many individuals use irrevocable life insurance trusts for estate tax reasons. If the irrevocable trust is drafted properly, it can possibly be used as a vehicle to provide a source of funding to pay the estate tax liability on the death of the insured. If the insured is married, then the irrevocable life insurance trust can provide for the liquidity on the second to die of the insured (husband and wife). That happens when the life insurance policy is a second-to-die policy.

According to the IRS rules, the trustee of the irrevocable trust cannot be obligated to pay the estate tax liability of the grantor or grantors of the irrevocable trust if a second-to-die policy is involved. If that provision is accidently included in the irrevocable trust document, then the IRS will include the policy proceeds in the estate of the insured or the estate of the second to die of the insureds, as the case may be, for estate tax purposes.

The irrevocable trust document can permit (not mandate) that the trustee of the irrevocable trust may purchase assets from the estate of the grantor or the estate of the second to die of the grantors, as the case may be, at fair market value. The irrevocable trust document can also permit the trustee of the irrevocable trust to lend money to the estate of the grantor or the estate of the second to die of the grantors, as the case may be, provided that the loan is adequately secured and a reasonable rate of interest is payable on the loan. The terms of the loan must be at arm's length and the trustee must be sure that the trust beneficiaries are adequately protected.

If the trustee is careless and does not protect the trust beneficiaries properly, then the trustee faces liability problems with the trust beneficiaries.

As the federal estate tax exemption increases as a result of the inflation adjustment, then the need for the irrevocable life insurance trust for federal estate tax purposes diminishes. State estate tax issues may or may not be significant enough to justify the use of the irrevocable life insurance trust for that reason alone.

However, the irrevocable life insurance trust can still be useful in passing assets down to children and grandchildren.

Asset protection is one of the main reasons for establishing an irrevocable life insurance trust, in addition to estate tax reasons.

If an irrevocable life insurance trust is used as a vehicle for generation-skipping purposes, then the generation-skipping transfer tax exemption available to the grantor can be used in order to avoid or minimize generation-skipping transfer taxes.

In addition, in a second-to-die policy situation, both the husband and wife can be grantors of the irrevocable life insurance policy and double up on the amount of the generation-skipping exemption that can be used in order to avoid or minimize generation-skipping transfer taxes.

Other approaches can be used to minimize generation-skipping transfer tax liabilities as well, even if the life insurance policy is a first-to-die policy.

LIVING TRUST SCAMS

There are many good reasons for establishing trusts. However, on occasion trusts are the subject of living trust scams involving senior citizens who are often confused about avoiding probate and instead use living trusts as a means for transferring assets to their heirs.

The following are examples of discussions regarding living trust scams taken from a number of sources.

Source: Washington State Office of the Attorney General

CONSUMER PROTECTION: SHUTTING DOWN "TRUST MILLS"

Background

"Trust mills" are used by salespeople who prey on seniors and convince them through scare tactics and deception that they need a living trust. While these salespeople are convincing a senior to purchase a trust—generally for $1,500–2,000—they are also gathering detailed information about the senior's assets, claiming they need it to prepare the trust. Instead most of these trusts are cookie-cutter documents prepared in bulk on a home computer. Once the trust is signed and delivered, the salesperson uses the relationship to sell other financial products, like reverse mortgages and annuities that may be unnecessary or even contrary to the senior's interests.

. . . , an early perpetrator of the scheme, sought out older widowed women and billed himself as a financial planning expert.

He held free seminars where he urged attendees to sign up for "free in-home consultations."

Then he used his relationship to systematically bilk his clients of their life savings.

61

The Attorney General's Office Consumer Protection Division obtained a civil judgment of more than $1 million against . . . , the Office of the Insurance Commissioner revoked his insurance license and he was finally convicted on securities fraud but he's now bankrupt and his clients will never fully recover from the financial harm he caused.

Typically, the price paid for a living trust through a trust mill is similar to the cost to buy one through a licensed attorney, however, the attorney has an enforceable professional obligation to provide accurate and appropriate estate planning advice.

The Attorney General's Office Consumer Protection Division has been bringing cases against living trust mills for more than a decade. The office generally has one or two of these cases on the docket at any given time, but for every case the office brings, our attorneys learn of several new operations they are unable to address due to limited resources and the complexity of the cases:

(1) The vulnerable senior victims generally have difficulty providing accurate testimony;

(2) Sometimes the harm caused by the trust mill isn't evident to the purchaser and may not come to light until after the senior has passed away and descendents [sic] learn the trust was ineffective or inappropriate;

(3) The defendant will claim they just "provided information" and will deny engaging in the practice of law;

(4) The time it takes to investigate and prosecute these cases allows for dissipation of the assets available to provide restitution to the victim.

Action:

Attorney General McKenna requested legislation to protect seniors from trust mill scams (HB 1114-Representatives Jay Rodne (R–Issaquah), Pat Lantz (D–Gig Harbor), Jim Moeller (D–Vancouver) and Brian Sullivan (D–Mukilteo) by prohibiting anyone other than attorneys or those employed by attorneys from marketing legal estate distribution documents like living trusts, wills, etc.

Attorneys who sell inappropriate living trusts will be accountable through bar sanctions. Trust mill activity becomes a per se violation of the Consumer Protection Act so the outcome of litigation against trust mill activity is substantially certain with greater clarity which will result in broad deterrence. Financial institutions are exempt.

This bill passed the Legislature and was signed by the Governor.

Source: Washington State Office of Attorney General

LIVING TRUSTS SCAMS

The living trust scam attempts to get you to purchase a trust. It plays on the fear that probate costs and estate taxes will erode the value of your estate. While living trusts can be a useful tool for some, many unscrupulous sales persons use it to simply get in the door and sell high-commission investments to consumers, whether or not it is the best thing for them.

THE OPENING PITCH

"Do you want to leave a legacy for your grandchildren and not have the government take all the money you have spent a lifetime saving? Come to a free seminar to learn how."

THE PRESENTATION

You respond to such a mailer, phone call or advertisement by attending a workshop. Or you might call to find out about it and someone will come out to your home to present information. They will sign you up for a living trust by having you fill out forms that disclose all of your financial assets. Once they have seen your finances, they begin to recommend different investments, usually insurance type products like annuities, in order to earn high commissions off the sale of those products.

THE RESULT

Sometimes the living trust document you buy is not filled out properly because lawyers are not doing it. If these documents are filled out improperly, you may end up going through probate anyway, the very thing you were told you could avoid. In addition, many older people end up buying investments that are not appropriate for them given their situation.

HOW TO AVOID IT

If you want to know if a living trust will truly help you, you should get the advice of an estate-planning attorney. You can find the name and phone number for such an attorney by calling your local bar association, lawyer referral service.

Source: State of California Department of Justice Office of the Attorney General

LIVING TRUST MILLS

Companies advertising "living trusts" sometimes misrepresent the advantages of living trusts. But the most serious problem is the misuse of the financial information sales persons obtain to prepare a living trust. Unfortunately, this information is used to sell unneeded annuities and various investments, most often to senior citizens.

Sales agents for these operations often misrepresent the disadvantages of seniors' current investments and the advantages of the investments the agents are selling. They may even make seniors believe their bank accounts are less safe than the annuities or other investments they want seniors to buy. To give themselves a cloak of legitimacy, these sales agents pretend to be experts in living trusts. In their solicitations, these sales agents often pose as expert financial or estate planners. They pass themselves off as a "trust adviser," "senior estate planner" or "paralegal," and schedule an initial appointment with seniors in their homes. Under the guise of helping set up or update a living trust, the sales agents find out about seniors' financial assets and investments. They sometimes work in assisted living centers, churches and other places where seniors gather, hooking elderly victims through free seminars and other sales presentations.

Seniors pay substantial sums of money to sales agents for living trusts, but sometimes, through fraud and deceit, the sales agents damage seniors' estate plans, and the security of their investments and life savings.

Usually, the sales agents schedule a home visit to explain the living trust and use a second visit to deliver a completed trust and have documents signed and notarized, and title of assets transferred to the trust. Typically, during the second visit, the agents go over the assets to be placed in the trust. The agents may have seniors sign documents that transfer the senior's CD, mutual fund accounts, or other investments to an annuity, or a so called "promissory note" or other investment. They use that review of seniors' investments to scare them into believing their investments are unsafe, and that by "moving" their money, they can earn higher interest with less risk. Frequently, there are substantial penalties for early withdrawal of the investment.

Planning an estate and choosing investments involve important legal, financial and personal decisions. If estate planning documents are not properly prepared or executed they can be invalid and cause lasting damage.

Following are tips to help consumers avoid becoming victims of living trust mills and their scams:

Living trust mills' sales agents are usually not attorneys and are not experts in estate planning.

Watch out for companies that sell trusts and also try to sell annuities or other investments.

Sales agents may fail to disclose possible adverse tax consequences or early withdrawal penalties that may be incurred when transferring stocks, bonds, certificates of deposit or other investments to annuities.

An annuity is not 100% safe, and only a portion is guaranteed by the state. Insurance companies can and do fail, and their assets may not be enough to pay the full value of their customers' investments.

So called "promissory notes" are not insured by the FDIC or any other government agency and may be very risky. They may not be registered as securities with the state.

Before consumers buy an annuity or any other investment, they should review it with people they know and trust, such as their financial or tax adviser, their attorney and trusted family members.

An attorney qualified in estate planning can help consumers decide if they need a living trust or other estate planning documents, or help them review an existing trust or will. To obtain a list of attorneys who are certified as estate planning specialists, and to receive other written information about estate planning and how to select an attorney, call the California State Bar's toll free number for seniors at 1-888-460-7364.

Consumers who feel they have been victimized by a living trust mill, or annuity or promissory note fraud, should report it to the Consumer Fraud Section of their local district attorney and to the California Department of Insurance. Consumers can also file complaints online at the Attorney General's website.

Source: State of California Attorney General Bill Lockyer

SCAM ALERT

LIVING TRUST / ANNUITY / AND PROMISSORY NOTE SCAMS

Living trust mills often solicit senior citizens by telephone, mail or seminars, offering "free" information about trusts, wills or taxes, or the need to update an existing trust. According to Attorney General Lockyer, "These trust mills often violate a number of California laws." He continues, "To give their unlawful businesses legitimacy in the eyes of seniors, living trust mills may offer to do free seminars or other programs at senior centers, assisted living centers, churches or other places where seniors gather."

HOW A LIVING TRUST MILL SCHEME WORKS

Sales agents, posing as expert estate or financial planners, often using bogus titles, such as "trust adviser," "senior estate planner," or "paralegal," then schedule follow-up appointments after the seminars with seniors in their homes. These agents are sales persons, not experts in estate planning, and they usually get paid high commissions on the trust packages and annuities that they sell. Their goal is to sell their products, not protect the interests of the senior.

Sales agents are not attorneys, but they may mention an attorney who supposedly prepares the trust and represents the senior's interests. An attorney may even appear at the seminar. But most victims never have a private consultation with an attorney who is an expert in estate planning or who reviews with them the various options for estate planning and considers the senior's desires and needs before a decision is made as to the type of estate plan needed. Often seniors never even talk with an attorney, and the attorney does not directly supervise the sales agents' activities.

Under the guise of helping the seniors to set up or update a living trust, the sales agents find out about the seniors' financial assets and investments. Seniors rarely understand that the so-called expert they begin to trust is using the living trust as a means of selling them an investment to replace the investments they presently have.

Usually, the sales agents schedule a second home visit to deliver a completed trust and have documents signed, title of assets transferred to the trust and various documents notarized. Typically, the agents go over the assets to be placed in the trust and use that review to scare seniors into believing that their investments are unsafe and that by "moving" their money, they can earn higher interest with no risk. These agents are often insurance agents who are really there to try to sell annuities. The agents may also try to sell so-called promissory notes or other investments. Agents may have the senior sign documents to transfer the senior's CD, mutual fund accounts or other investments to these other investments.

Documents, prepared by Living Trust Mill agents, may not comply with California law, or agents may not follow procedures set by law for executing or witnessing wills and other documents, which can make the documents subject to challenge. Agents often misrepresent the value of a trust, the disadvantages of the senior's current investments, and the advantages of the investments the agents are selling.

The trust mill may not properly have assets "funded" or transferred into the trust. Sales agents may fail to disclose possible adverse tax consequences or early withdrawal penalties that may be incurred when transferring stocks, bonds, certificates of deposit or other investments to annuities, so-called promissory notes or other investments offered by agents.

Sales agents may fail to disclose substantial surrender penalties that apply on death or if an annuity is canceled during the first 5 to 10 years, or more, of a proposed annuity.

Agents may even make seniors believe their bank accounts are less safe than the annuities or other investments the agents are selling. They may falsely claim that no one has ever lost any money in an annuity, that annuities are fully guaranteed by the state or that annuities are safe. Annuities are not 100% safe and only a portion is guaranteed by the state. Insurance companies can and do fail, and their assets may not be enough to pay the full value of their customer's investments.

So-called "promissory notes" are not insured by the FDIC or any other government agency and may be very risky. They may not even be registered as securities with the state. These companies are often not regulated. They can and do fail, and there may be few or no assets left to repay investors.

HOW TO AVOID THE LIVING TRUST MILL SCAM

Lockyer says, "Planning an estate involves important financial and personal decisions. If wills, trusts, powers of attorney or other estate planning documents are not properly prepared or executed they can be invalid and cause lasting damage."

Do not resort to services offered by these living trust mills at seminars, by telemarketing or mail solicitations.

Obtain a list of attorneys, who are certified as estate planning specialists, by calling the State Bar of California's toll-free number for seniors: 1-888-460-7364.

Receive written information about estate planning and how to select an attorney by calling the State Bar at 1-888-460-7364. (The State Bar also offers a videotape for use with senior groups that demonstrates common living trust scams and how to avoid them.)

Before buying an annuity or any other investment, or before withdrawing money from an existing investment, the Attorney General recommends seniors get copies of the sales offer and documents and review them with people they know and trust, such as their financial or tax adviser, their attorney and trusted family members before they sign anything.

WHAT TO DO IF YOU BELIEVE YOU MAY ALREADY HAVE BEEN VICTIMIZED

Report it to your local district attorney and the California Department of Insurance OR call the Attorney General's Public Inquiry Unit at 1-800-952-5225. Consumer complaints may also be filed on-line at the Attorney General's website at http://www.ag.ca.gov/consumers/general.htm

Source: the State of Michigan Attorney General

LIVING TRUSTS

Beware of "One Size Fits All" Estate Plans & "Free Lunch Seminars"
CONSUMER ALERT
BILL SCHUETTE
ATTORNEY GENERAL

The Attorney General provides Consumer Alerts to inform the public of unfair, misleading, or deceptive business practices, and to provide information and guidance on other issues of concern. Consumer Alerts are not legal advice, legal authority, or a binding legal opinion from the Department of Attorney General.

LIVING TRUSTS

Beware of "One Size Fits All" Estate Plans & "Free Lunch Seminars"

Misinformation about the cost and complexity of probate provides a golden opportunity for sales pitches exploiting fears that life savings may be lost to taxes, predatory probate attorneys, or distributed years after death because of court delays. With laws curbing telemarketing sales calls, use of free lunch seminars to pitch estate planning products have surged. Promoted as "educational" programs, these seminars are commonly a sales job in disguise. Be alert to seminars pushing "one size fits all" estate planning products, including living trusts. A decision as important as estate planning should be made with reliable, professional counsel who can help you decide what estate plan is best for your own individual situation, rather than someone whose primary interest is making a sale.

WHAT IS A LIVING TRUST?

A revocable living trust is created for the purpose of holding ownership to an individual's assets during the person's lifetime, and for distributing those assets after death. It is called a "living trust" because it is created and takes effect during the maker's lifetime, in contrast to a will, which does not take effect until after the death of its maker. The individual who creates the living trust (the grantor) gives control of his or her property to a trust, which is administered by the "trustee" for the "beneficiary's" benefit. The grantor, trustee and beneficiary may be the same person, with a successor trustee named to distribute assets after death.

A living trust is a legitimate estate planning device that for some people can be a useful and practical tool. But for others, it can be a waste of time and money, and not appropriate to individual estate planning needs. Contrary to some sales pitches, not everyone benefits from a living trust. Estate planning choices should be discussed with experienced estate planning professionals, including your attorney and financial planner.

TIPS TO REMEMBER ABOUT FREE LUNCH SEMINARS

Never assume that a seminar is purely informational, even if it is held in a public place such as a library or senior center. Seminars are often designed to sell—either at the seminar itself or later—with sign-in sheets often used to make future sales calls. Attending a seminar may lead to a high pressure in-home sales pitch.

Seminar speakers may be biased in their 'estate planning' recommendations. A seminar is commonly funded with the expectation that the sponsor's products will be sold to attendees.

Seminar content and materials may be misleading, with exaggerated claims about the length and cost of probate and the purported advantages of living trusts.

"Experts" may misrepresent their qualifications. The education, experience, and other requirements for receiving a "senior" designation vary greatly and in some cases may be a marketing tool.

Product recommendations must be suitable for you. Be wary of "one size fits all" recommendations.

TIPS TO HELP IN MAKING A WISE DECISION BEFORE PURCHASING A LIVING TRUST

Do not be pressured into purchasing a trust based on the in-home sales pitch of a salesman, or immediately following a seminar. Before making any purchase decision, consult with an independent and reliable professional with the necessary background to help you decide what estate plan is best for your individual situation. If you already have a lawyer, discuss the living trust offer with him or her before buying.

Do not take the word of a sales agent as to whether a living trust is the best estate plan for you. The selection of the appropriate estate plan for your circumstances should not be based on the representations of a person whose primary interest is in making a sale of his company's estate plan product, and who is not a lawyer or reliable estate planning professional. If the sales agent says that the purchase price will include consultation with an attorney, wait until after the promised attorney consultation to select and pay for the estate plan.

Before buying a living trust from a stranger, call a local lawyer and ask him or her what they charge for preparing trusts. Often the price is much higher than what a local lawyer would charge. Companies selling living trusts rely on the public's apprehension that attorneys are costly.

Be wary if a trust salesperson promises specific results or dollar savings. Costs of probate and attorney fees vary greatly from state to state, and according to personal circumstances.

Check out trust company lawyers with the State Bar of Michigan. If the trust salesperson promises a lawyer will review the customer's documents, demand the name of the lawyer and check with the State Bar of Michigan to make certain the lawyer is licensed to practice in Michigan.

If the salesperson gives the impression that his or her company or the living trust being sold is recommended or endorsed by AARP, do not buy! AARP does not endorse or recommend any living trust product at this time.

Do not give personal or confidential family and financial information to a salesperson, even if the salesperson promises it will be passed on to a licensed lawyer. Meet with or discuss the matter with the lawyer personally.

Watch out for companies that sell trusts and also try to sell annuities or other investment. Under the guise of setting up a living trust, financial information disclosed to salespeople may be used to sell financial products, such as annuities. In some instances, the real goal of the living trust sale is to gain access to asset information in order that sales agents can earn high commissions by "moving" existing investments into others being sold by the living trust company.

If the salesperson says part of the trust cost will pay the lawyer's fee, do not buy! A lawyer may not split a fee with the salesperson or the trust company.

Discuss whether you can get your money back if you are not satisfied, and get the promise in writing.

If you have already purchased a living trust without personal consultation with an attorney, have the living trust document reviewed by a reliable attorney. Make sure that the living trust document will achieve your intended estate planning goals. Unscrupulous living trust sales people may charge thousands of dollars for what amounts to a set of pre-printed legal forms. In some instances, because all consumers are sold the same package, the living trust may be ill-suited or even contrary to individual estate planning needs.

To file a complaint against a person or business that sells living trusts, Consumers may contact the Attorney General's Consumer Protection Division at:

Consumer Protection Division
P.O. Box 30213
Lansing, MI 48909
517-373-1140
Fax: 517-241-3771
Toll free: 877-765-8388
www.michigan.gov/ag (online complaint form)

To complain about an attorney who is part of a living trust sales promotion, or non-lawyers engaged in the unauthorized practice of law, please contact:

State Bar of Michigan
306 Townsend St.
Lansing, MI 48933
(517) 346-6300

Source: Office of the Minnesota Attorney General

LIVING TRUSTS

Senior citizens are often targeted by unscrupulous salespeople who instill and prey on seniors' financial fears in order to sell unwanted, unnecessary and/or unsuitable living trusts, legal plans, and other financial products. Seniors should use extreme caution when approached by individuals trying to sell these types of products.

Living trusts organize your financial situation, and living wills spell out your health care wishes. The two are often confused. Scam artists play on the fact that seniors are not familiar with living trusts, so they advertise presentations at hotels or restaurants or come to your door with information to teach you about financial options, including trusts. Protect yourself. Watch for the following clues:

A salesperson requests highly personal financial information.

A salesperson, untrained in the law, tells you need a trust or makes misleading statements about trusts such as: "A trust will protect your estate from inheritance taxes."

Thousands of dollars are charged for boilerplate forms.

The sales pitch grossly emphasizes the need to avoid probate and grossly exaggerates the estimate of probate cost.

Do not put your financial future into the hands of a door-to-door salesperson. Consult an attorney or financial planner who specializes in estate planning, or contact the Senior Federation legal referral program.

RESOURCES

Minnesota Attorney General's Office
   Consumer Protection
   445 Minnesota Street, Suite 1400
   St. Paul, MN 55101
   Helpline: (651) 296-3353
   1-800-657-3787
   TTY: (651) 297-7206
   TTY: 1-800-366-4812

Senior Linkage Line
   Minnesota Board on Aging
   (651)431-2500
   1-800-333-2433

Better Business Bureau
   220 South River Ridge Circle
   Burnsville, MN 55337
   651-699-1111
   1-800-646-6222

www.bbb.org

Charities Review Council
2610 University Avenue West, Suite 375
St. Paul, MN 55114-2007
651-224-7030 or 1-800-733-4483
www.smartgivers.org

Minnesota Department of Commerce
85 East 7th Place, Suite 500
St. Paul, MN 55101
(651) 539-1500
www.commerce.state.mn.us

Do-Not-Call List Registration
(888)382-1222
(866)290-4236(TTY)
www.donotcall.gov

Handbook Provides Additional Information

Seniors' Legal Rights is a comprehensive publication designed to inform older people of their rights on a number of topics, ranging from consumer protection and estate planning to utilities and nursing homes. To order a copy please contact the Attorney General's Office at the address and phone numbers above.

Source: Office of Minnesota Attorney General Lori Swanson

Not everyone needs or can benefit from a living trust. Under Minnesota law, personal property and estates under $50,000 do not need to go through formal probate. There are other ways to transfer assets to someone else without being probated, such as holding a home in joint tenancy, having joint bank accounts, or listing a person as a beneficiary. Estates under $1 million are not subject to estate taxes under Minnesota law, so a trust will not help those estates save in estate taxes. A living trust may impact your ability to qualify for Medical Assistance should it be necessary if you need long term or nursing home care. And if you have a living trust, if you fail to transfer all property into the trust, that property still must be probated.

A Hidden Agenda

In the course of asking you about your estate wishes, the trust salesman will obtain a lot of financial data about you. He will ask you how much money you have in the bank and where your investments and insurance are held. Unknown to you at the time, this "estate planning specialist" is likely an insurance salesman (or someone who works with an insurance salesman). He usually won't try to sell you insurance at the first meeting—because that would be a red flag for you; instead, he will try to build your trust over several meetings. He (or the person that delivers your completed trust documents) will usually try to sell you annuities or insurance at a later appointment, with the benefit of already having complete information about your finances.

Annuities are complex products. If you move your money from another product, you may have to pay fees or penalties. Some long-term annuities may lock up your money for more than ten years, subjecting you to penalties if you need to access your money for living expenses. Annuities sometimes also have complicated interest-crediting provisions, leading to confusion about how much interest you will earn. Take time to think over the purchase of annuities or insurance—talk to family, friends, or an experienced local investment professional.

How to Protect Yourself

Be suspicious of ads for "free" dinners or workshops and salespeople who call you on the telephone to sell you estate planning advice. This adage holds true: "There is no such thing as a free lunch." The people who hold these "free" dinners want to sell you something—often a trust followed by annuities, insurance or investments.

If you want a will, trust, or estate plan, seek out an experienced local attorney. To play it safe, the attorney should be somebody you seek out, not someone who finds you. People who call and write you want to sell you something.

Living trust mills may use non-attorneys or out-of-state attorneys to draft your will. Under Minnesota law, non-Minnesota attorneys are not supposed to draft trusts and wills for residents of Minnesota.

Estate plan salesmen use high-pressure tactics. They may tell you they're only in town for a few days or may make you feel guilty because they have spent so much time at your kitchen table. These are big decisions, and you should take time to think about them and consult with a professional or trusted family member or friend. Remember: it is not impolite to say that you're not interested.

Minnesota law generally allows three business days to cancel most sales made in your home. The company is required to notify you of your right to do this using certain forms and language. If you get into a bad situation you regret, cancel right away in writing and keep a copy for your records.

Office of Minnesota Attorney General Lori Swanson
1400 Bremer Tower
445 Minnesota Street
St. Paul, MN 55101
(651) 296-3353
1-800-657-3787
TTY: (651) 297-7206
TTY: 1-800-366-4812
Source: Pennsylvania Attorney General

BEWARE OF LIVING TRUST SCAMS

Planning in advance for the distribution of assets at death is a good idea. While there are many ways to do this, in order to make the right decision the smart consumer needs to explore every option and consider the type of estate planning that's appropriate for them. One device is a living trust which is a trust set up during a person's lifetime. This may be a good idea for some, but not for others. Most importantly, keep in mind that when considering your estate planning needs, your interests may best be met by consulting with an attorney.

What is a trust?

A trust is a written legal document into which you (the Trustor) place some or all of your asset. The assets are managed by you or whomever you designate until your death or a specific date set by you.

Can I change my mind or add/delete items I place in the Trust?

These are details which you would choose upon creation of the Trust. A REVOCABLE (able to be cancelled or altered) TRUST can be changed which is different from an IRREVOCABLE TRUST, which cannot be changed.

What amount of assets are needed in order for a Trust to be right for me?

The dollar value of assets is a very important factor when considering a Living Trust, however it is only one factor. Consult a licensed attorney specializing in Trusts and Estates (PA Bar Association www.PaBar.org) or contact the Pennsylvania Securities commission www.psc.state.pa.us.

THE SCAMS

Unfortunately, when it comes to living trusts, unscrupulous con artists are ready to play on consumers' fears of the unknown. In some cases, consumers—mostly elderly—are solicited by phone or mail to attend seminars or to set up in-home appointments to discuss living trusts. Living trusts are then marketed through high-pressure sales pitches which prey on the fear that assets will be tied up indefinitely or that estates are prone to heavy taxes and fees if a living trust is not in place. Con artists often rely on unfamiliar terms such as "probate" and "executor" to convince consumers that a living trust is right for them even though many of the complex rules and fees that can complicate estate distributions do not exist in Pennsylvania.

Sometimes victims are sold worthless "kits," costing several thousand dollars, which are nothing more than standard forms that may or may not be valid, as laws concerning living trusts vary from state to state. In other cases, false promoters simply want to gain access to consumers' financial information so they can sell them other products, like insurance annuities.

THE FACTS

To avoid being taken advantage of by these con artists, keep the following tips in mind:

Shop around. Check out offers with a trusted attorney or estate planner.

Be certain a living trust is the best option for your situation.

Never sign anything containing options or terminology you don't understand.

Do not give in to high-pressure sales tactics. Legitimate offers will be around long enough for you to properly research them.

Always check out offers from telephone solicitors or door-to-door sales people.

Make sure you have the option of updating your trust periodically. Understand how this is done and be aware of any costs incurred to do so.

Beware of anyone portraying living trusts as being a solution for estate planning.

Verify any stated affiliation or endorsement by a government agency or senior association.

The Cooling Off Rule states that if you buy a living trust in your home or somewhere other than the seller's permanent place of business (like a hotel seminar), you have three business days to cancel the deal.

TERMINOLOGY TO UNDERSTAND

Grantor—You are the Grantor since you convey or transfer ownership from you to the Trust. For example, "The Trust of John Smith" is the owner of the real estate or personal property within the trust you created.

Beneficiary—Person(s), corporations, non-profit organizations or whomever you designate.

Fiduciary—An individual or trust company that is for the benefit of another. Also, known as trustees, executor/executrix, or representative are all fiduciaries

Probate—A will, whether single or within a Trust, is subject to review and authentication by the Register of Wills, in the county where the descendant resided at a primary residence.

If you have any questions, or want to file a complaint, call the Attorney General's Bureau of Consumer Protection hotline: 1-800-441-2555, or visit our website at www.attorneygeneral.gov.

Source: Attorney General of Texas Greg Abbott

BEWARE OF UNETHICAL SALES OF LIVING TRUSTS, ANNUITIES

As Attorney General, I urge seniors to exercise great caution when considering living trusts. For the vast majority of seniors, a living trust is NOT likely to be preferable to a will and a durable power of attorney. Each person should consult a Texas attorney who is experienced in estate planning to analyze whether or not a living trust is appropriate for them, because the decision depends on each person's individual circumstances.

Living trusts are often sold using false or misleading information about the benefits they offer or by representations that everyone needs a living trust. Some con artists charge as much as $1,800 for a living trust and will try to talk you into the sale without regard to whether it is really appropriate for you. You should be particularly wary of a person who is selling living trusts from door to door and of attorneys and financial advisers recommended by them.

You should also be cautious about allowing a living trust salesperson to see your assets and your net worth. If you are subsequently contacted by a salesperson offering annuity products, you should be aware that there are several types of annuities, which may or may not be appropriate for seniors as a tool for financial planning. For more information about living trusts and other forms of advance planning, visit the Senior Texans Page of our Web site.

General Abbott's signature
Greg Abbott
Attorney General of Texas

IRAS PAYABLE TO
NON-QTIP IRA TRUSTS
(THE GOOD, THE BAD, AND THE UGLY)

Many taxpayers often have retirement assets such as IRAs payable to trusts. These trusts can be revocable trusts, irrevocable trusts, or trusts under a will.

If done correctly, these trusts can in essence result in a windfall for the trust beneficiary and provide him or her with a long-term benefit. However, if done incorrectly or if the trust flunks the IRS rules, including the IRS final regulations and rulings, then it can be a time bomb with devastating problems for the trustee and possibly the professional adviser who is involved in the creation of the trust and/or the compliance aspects of the trust after the death of the IRA owner or employee plan participant whose retirement account or IRA account is payable to a trust.

An IRA trust can generally provide for protection against the creditors of the trust beneficiary and prevent the trust from being included in the trust beneficiary's estate for estate tax purposes if the trust beneficiary dies during the payout period. In addition, the IRA trust can be used as a generation-skipping vehicle and also as a credit shelter trust if done correctly.

In the event that the IRA trust is nonqualifying (a trust that does not satisfy the IRS stretch payment rules), then significant tax problems and other liability issues may be triggered. This can become a problem for the trustee and possibly the trustee's advisers as well. *Please review the situations described in this section for additional pitfall issues.*

There are a number of problems that exist from a legal point of view when drafting an IRA trust. If a practitioner is not versed in the state trust law that defines income and principal, then the trust document may be written in a manner that is inconsistent with the intent of the grantor.

For example, if the IRA trust provides that income shall be paid to the trust beneficiary each year, then one must examine the definition of income when a required minimum distribution is paid to the trust under state law. Many of the states have adopted a version of the 1997 UPAIA. In a non-QTIP IRA trust, the definition of income in most (but not all) adopting jurisdictions of the 1997 version of the UPAIA is 10 percent of the required minimum distribution amount received by the trust. In that case, if the required minimum distribution payable to the IRA trust is $30,000, then the trust beneficiary will receive only 10 percent of $30,000, or $3,000, not $30,000. However, if the trust provision provides that Joey, the nonspouse trust beneficiary, shall receive the greater of income or the required minimum distribution that the trust receives each year, then Joey will receive $30,000, not $3,000. If the trust states only that Joey receives income (not the greater of income or the required minimum distribution amount), then if Joey was erroneously paid $30,000 instead of $3,000, the trustee has a significant legal problem. The trustee would have to advise the trust beneficiary, Joey, that he was overpaid by $27,000. This overpayment can lead to headaches for the trustee if Joey paid income taxes on the $30,000 amount and spent the remaining money.

Many other drafting issues must be covered in the trust document as well. For example, if the IRA trust provides for the payment of trust expenses (which it should and generally does), then trust expenses are generally charged against trust income under state trust law. However, if the trust income is only 10 percent of the required minimum distribution amount, then it may not be sufficient to support the payment of trust expenses. For that reason, I suggest that a non-QTIP trust provide that any trust expenses be charged against principal, not income. In that connection, when a non-QTIP IRA trust is used, I suggest that the trust provide that all distributions received by the trust from the decedent's IRA be considered principal and that the trustee shall accelerate distributions from the IRA to the trust in order to pay the trustee expenses, which are also charged against principal. The author does not offset the trust expenses against the required minimum distribution amount payable to Joey even though an IRS letter ruling permits the netting approach. An

IRS letter ruling granted to a particular taxpayer is not binding on the IRS with respect to any other taxpayer.

Once an IRA trust is established, the beneficiary form with the IRA institution should indicate, for example, that the Harvey trust f/b/o Marty dated July 1, 2013, is the primary beneficiary of Harvey's IRA *provided* that Marty survives Harvey. It should also indicate that if Marty does not survive Harvey, the contingent beneficiaries of Harvey's IRA are Mary and Tommy or the survivor of them, for example.

I recommend that the Harvey trust f/b/o Marty be conditioned on the survival of Marty. Most canned IRA beneficiary forms just provide for the trust to be the beneficiary of Harvey's IRA. That could be a headache if for some reason Marty predeceased Harvey and Harvey died or became legally incompetent before he had a chance to change the IRA beneficiary form.

In order for the IRA trust for the benefit of Marty to be able to use the life expectancy of Marty after Harvey's death, the trustee of Harvey's trust must satisfy one of the IRS post death trust documentation requirements by no later than October 31 following the year of death of the IRA owner. This assumes that the trust was drafted properly and otherwise satisfies the IRS rules.

The IRS post death trust documentation requirements are found at Reg. Sec. 1.401(a)(9)-4, A-6(b). One method of satisfying the IRS rules requires that certain detailed statements be made by the trustee and be timely sent by the trustee to the IRA institution. The second alternative method provides that a copy of the trust (including all amendments) be timely sent by the trustee to the IRA institution. In either case, the statute of limitations for compliance with the IRS post death trust documentation requirement must be satisfied by no later than October 31 following the year of death of the IRA owner.

If the IRA trust is drafted in a manner that flunks the IRS stretch payment rules, then the IRS will have a field day and possibly collect a significant amount of penalties. In addition, if the IRA trust is drafted properly but the IRS post death trust documentation requirement is not timely satisfied, then that is also a disaster.

Flunking the IRS trust stretch payment rules can be a nightmare for the trustee, the trust beneficiary, the trust remainderman, the trust accountant, and the trust counsel.

The following are examples on how to flunk the IRS rules without really trying.

SITUATION 1

Charlie, an attorney, drafts what he thinks is a valid IRA trust for his client, Harvey. The primary trust beneficiary of the IRA trust is Marty, who is age 12 in 2013. The beneficiary of Harvey's IRA is Harvey's trust for the benefit of Marty.

Under the terms of the Harvey trust, Marty will receive trust income until he attains age 35. Upon attainment of age 35, Marty is entitled to the trust principal. However, under the terms of the trust, in the event that Marty dies prior to the attainment of age 35, then the trust remainder is payable to the XYZ Charity.

Harvey dies in 2016 at age 67. In the calendar year 2017, Marty is age 16. Assume that the trustee of Harvey's trust sent a copy of Harvey's trust to the IRA financial institution prior to the October 31, 2017, deadline.

Question: Over what period will Harvey's trust receive required minimum distributions from Harvey's IRA?

Answer: Harvey's trust will receive required minimum distributions from Harvey's deceased IRA under the IRS five-year rule and not under IRS life expectancy stretch payout rules because of certain technical violations described in the Author's Note that follows.

Under the five-year rule, Harvey's deceased IRA account must be paid out to Harvey's trust by no later than December 31 of the end of the fifth year following the year of the IRA owner's death. That date is December 31, 2021.

Since Harvey died in 2016 at age 67, then the December 31 date that falls at the end of the fifth year following his year of death in 2016 is December 31, 2021.

Author's Note

The IRS five-year rule applies if the IRA owner dies before his or her required beginning date without having a designated beneficiary. Harvey died at age 67, before his required beginning date. A trust is not a designated beneficiary for purposes of determining in life expectancy payout rules. However, an individual beneficiary of a trust can be considered to be a designated beneficiary for purposes of the IRS life expectancy rules if the trust satisfies the IRS rules. The required beginning date for an IRA owner is April 1 of the calendar year following the year in which the IRA owner attains age 70½.

Although Marty is the primary beneficiary of the trust, he is not considered a designated beneficiary of the trust for IRS stretch payout purposes based on the facts in Situation 1. A designated beneficiary of a trust is an individual beneficiary whose life expectancy is used in determining the required minimum distributions that are made to the trust.

According to the trust document, Marty is an income beneficiary of Harvey's trust. Under state trust law, an income beneficiary is not the same as the beneficiary of required minimum distributions. In most states, only 10 percent of a required minimum distribution payment is considered income under state trust law. If Marty is an income beneficiary, then under the IRS rules, the life expectancy of the oldest trust remainderman is taken into account. Since the XYZ Charity is the trust remainderman, then the trustee has problems because a charity is not considered to be a designated beneficiary and has no life expectancy. Since Harvey died before his required beginning date without having a designated beneficiary for IRS purposes, then the five-year rule is operative. See IRS letter ruling 9820021 dated February 18, 1998, for the first ruling on this issue.

In the event that Harvey's IRA is not paid out to Harvey's trust by December 31, 2021, then to the extent that Harvey's IRA remains unpaid at that date, the Harvey trust is subject to a 50 percent excise tax on the unpaid amount.

If Harvey's IRA account as of December 31, 2021, is $200,000, then the IRS may impose a 50 percent penalty, or $100,000 ($200,000 x 50 percent), on the unpaid amount against the payee, Harvey's trust.

This 50 percent penalty may be asserted by the IRS at any time after the deadline of December 31, 2021, since, according to the Tax Court in *Paschall v. Comm.*, 137 T.C. No. 2, July 5, 2011, there is no statute of limitations if IRS Form 5329 is not filed with the IRS indicating the IRA penalty item. Although the *Paschall* case involved an IRA excess contribution issue under IRC Sec. 4973, it would also apply to IRC Sec. 4974. IRC Sec. 4974 provides for a 50 percent excise tax in a shortfall in a required minimum distribution payment.

In the event, for example, that the IRS examined the Harvey trust return in 2026, then the IRS could assess a 50 percent excise tax of $100,000 retroactively to 2021 against the Harvey trust based on the *Paschall* case. This could happen because the Harvey trust never filed a Form 5329 informing the IRS as to the shortfall amount of $200,000 for the calendar year ending December 31, 2021. In addition, the IRS could assert a delinquency penalty of 25 percent because of the failure to timely file a Form 5329.

Best Practice

The trustee of the Harvey trust should voluntarily file a Form 5329 as soon as possible after finding out about the shortfall and ask for a waiver of the 50 percent excise tax. In order to obtain a waiver, the trustee of the Harvey trust should close out the Harvey deceased IRA account as soon as possible and report the distribution as income to the trust in the year received. The trustee of Harvey's trust should then apply to the IRS for a waiver of the 50 percent excise tax on the Form 5329 for the calendar year ending December 31, 2021, and attach a detailed explanation as to the reasons why the shortfall took place and the steps taken to correct the error.

If the IRS finds the shortfall in a required minimum distribution on an examination, then it may be more difficult to obtain a waiver of the 50 percent excise tax after the fact. A voluntary disclosure before the fact is the best practice.

SITUATION 2

Assume the facts in Situation 1 except that the trustee of the Harvey trust has the discretion to accelerate distributions from Harvey's IRA for purposes of the health, education, maintenance, and support of Marty.

Question: Would your answer to Situation 1 change?

Answer: No. According to IRS letter ruling 9820021 dated February 18, 1998, the IRA trust is still a nonqualifying trust. The terms of the Harvey trust do not mandate that the required minimum distributions be paid to Marty. Any discretion granted to the trustee to accelerate distributions is not relevant since the trustee is not required to pay Marty the required minimum distributions.

SITUATION 3

Assume the facts in Situation 2 except that the terms of the trust provide that Marty is to receive the greater of income or required minimum distributions each year.

Question: Would your answer to Situation 2 change?

Answer: Maybe. The IRS regulations still require that the IRS post death trust documentation requirement be timely satisfied with the IRA institution by no later than October 31 of the year following the IRA owner's death. If it was timely satisfied, then the answer is yes. If it was not, then the answer is no.

Author's Note

In order to use the life expectancy of a trust beneficiary in determining required minimum distributions that must be made to the trust, then the rules found in Reg. Sec. 1.401(a)(9)-4, A-5 and Reg. Sec. 1.401(a)(9)-4, A-6(b) must be satisfied.

The following are some of the points reflected in these regulations:

1. A trust is not considered to be a designated beneficiary.

Continued

Continued:

2. The individual beneficiary of the trust may be considered to be a designated beneficiary [if the trust is drafted correctly] and the IRS trust documentation requirement is timely satisfied with the IRA institution].

3. The life expectancy of the appropriate individual beneficiary of the trust will be used in determining the required minimum distributions that must be made to the trust.

4. The trust must satisfy a number of additional rules under the IRS regulations. These rules follow:

1. The trust is a valid trust under state law, or would be but for the fact that there is no corpus.

2. The trust is irrevocable or will, by its terms, become irrevocable upon the death of the [IRA owner].

3. The beneficiaries of the trust who are beneficiaries to the trust's interest in the [IRA owner's] benefits are identifiable . . . from the trust instrument.

4. The documentation . . . has been [timely] provided to the [IRA institution].

* * *

Author's Note

The IRS post death trust documentation requirement must be satisfied with the IRA institution by no later than October 31 following the year of death of the IRA owner. The October 31 requirement is found in Reg. Sec. 1.401(a)(9)-4, A-6(b). Under the IRS rule, the trustee of the trust must either:

1. Provide the [IRA institution] with a final list of all beneficiaries of the trust (including contingent and remainderman beneficiaries with a description of the conditions on their entitlement) as of September 30 of the calendar year following the calendar year of the [IRA owner's] death; certify that, to the best of the trustee's knowledge, this list is correct and complete and that [certain other requirements] are satisfied; and agree to provide a copy of the trust instrument to the [IRA institution] upon demand; or

2. Provide the [IRA institution] with a copy of the actual trust document [including any amendments] for the trust that is named as a beneficiary of the [IRA owner] under the [IRA agreement] as of the [IRA owner's] date of death.

* * *

Author's Note

In practice, I use the second method. I have the trustee send a letter to the IRA institution together with the attached trust document and any amendments thereto, if any, well before the October 31 deadline.

This letter and attachment should be saved forever since an IRS agent on an audit of the IRA trust may request proof that the October 31 deadline was in fact met.

The trustee should send the letter and the attached trust document and amendments thereto, if any, to the IRA institution by certified mail, return receipt requested.

Further, additional copies of the transmittal letter and attachments should be maintained by the trustee, trust beneficiary, trust attorney, and trust accountant to play it safe.

---

* * *

Author's Note

Please avoid the drafting problem described in Situation 1 and Situation 2 when drafting an IRA trust.

SITUATION 4

Assume that the Harvey trust document provides that Marty receives the greater of income or the required minimum distributions from Harvey's trust each year. Further assume that the IRA trust was timely provided to the IRA institution prior to the October 31, 2017, deadline. Since Harvey died in 2016, the IRS post death trust documentation requirement must be satisfied with the IRA institution by October 31 following the year of Harvey's death.

Question: Over what term-certain period does Harvey's trust receive the required minimum distributions from Harvey's IRA?

Answer: Since Marty is age 16 in 2017, then the trustee uses Marty's IRS single life expectancy as determined in the calendar year following

Harvey's year of death in determining the required minimum distributions that are received by Harvey's trust from Harvey's IRA.

Under the IRS single life expectancy table, an individual age 16 has a 66.9-year term-certain period. The trustee uses this term-certain period.

Author's Note

The trustee of Harvey's trust receives the required minimum distribution from Harvey's IRA commencing in 2017 based on a term-certain period of 66.9 years and then remits the required minimum distribution amount to a custodian for Marty under the Uniform Gifts to Minors Act until Marty is age 21. This custodian provision should be incorporated in Harvey's trust agreement in the event that Marty is under the age of 21 at the time he is entitled to receive required minimum distributions. Please note that some jurisdictions may use age 18 instead of age 21. State law should be reviewed in that connection. In order to determine the amount of the required minimum distribution that must be received by Harvey's trust in 2017, the following formula is used: divide Harvey's deceased IRA account as of December 31, 2016, by 66.9. The result is the required minimum distribution for the calendar year 2017. For the calendar year 2018, Harvey's deceased IRA account as of December 31, 2017, is divided by 65.9. The result is the required minimum distribution for the calendar year 2018. That process is continued for each year thereafter.

Situation 5

Assume that the trustee of Harvey's trust sends the trust document to the IRA institution during Harvey's lifetime. However, the trustee of Harvey's trust mistakenly does not send a copy of the IRA trust to the IRA institution *post death* by the October 31 deadline following Harvey's year of death. Remember that Harvey died in 2016 at age 67. Also assume that the trust provides that Marty receives the greater of income or the required minimum distribution amount each year.

Question: May the trustee receive required minimum distributions from Harvey's trust based on the life expectancy of Marty as determined in the calendar year 2017?

Answer: No. The failure to satisfy the IRS post death trust documentation requirement with the IRA institution by the October 31, 2017, deadline is fatal. In that event, the IRA trust flunks the IRS life expectancy rule. Accordingly, the trustee of Harvey's trust must receive the entire proceeds of Harvey's IRA by no later than December 31, 2021, under the five-year rule in order to avoid the IRS 50 percent penalty on any shortfall amount. *Please note that Harvey died before his required beginning date, at age 67.* Because the trust flunks the IRS post death trust document requirement, then he is deemed to have died before his required beginning date without a designated beneficiary, according to the IRS rules. Therefore, the Harvey trust must receive Harvey's IRA under the five-year rule. In this case, the Harvey trust may not use the IRS life expectancy rule.

Situation 6

Assume that the IRA trust provisions provide that Marty shall receive the greater of income or required minimum distributions each year. Also assume that the IRS post death trust documentation requirement was timely satisfied with the IRA institution by the October 31 deadline (October 31, 2017).

Question: Does it matter that the XYZ Charity is the remainderman of the Harvey trust on the death of Marty from the IRS's point of view?

Answer: No. If Marty must receive the greater of income or required minimum distributions from the Harvey trust each year, then the IRS single life expectancy of Marty as determined in 2017 is used. The trust remainderman is not considered in that determination. The term-certain period that is used in determining required minimum distributions to the Harvey trust is 66.9 years.

Situation 7

Assume that Marty dies in January 2036 before receiving his required minimum distribution from the Harvey trust for the calendar year 2036. Assume that the amount involved is $100,000.

Question: Who receives the required minimum distribution for the calendar year 2036, Marty's estate or the XYZ Charity?

Answer: There is no IRS letter ruling on this point that I am aware of. The answer would depend on a construction proceeding by the court having jurisdiction of the Harvey trust.

In that case, Marty's estate would demand it and the XYZ Charity would demand it. The answer would then be determined by the court or by a settlement. If Harvey's trust stated that Marty would receive the entire required minimum distribution for each year that he was alive, then Marty's estate should win.

I suggest that the attorney draftsman cover that issue. An approach I use is to provide that to the extent that the required minimum distribution amount with respect to Marty's year of death is received by the Harvey trust prior to Marty's date of death and not paid to Marty prior to his date of death, then to that extent such amount shall be paid to the estate of Marty, and any and all required minimum distributions that are received by the Harvey trust on or after Marty's date of death shall be paid to the trust remaindermen.

Situation 8

Janet, an IRA owner, creates an IRA trust on October 1, 2011, for the benefit of her grandchild, Amy. The beneficiary of Janet's IRA is the Janet trust. According to the terms of the Janet trust, upon the death of Janet, the trustee of the Janet trust will make discretionary distributions to Amy until she attains age 30, at which time Amy shall have the right to withdraw the entire balance in Janet's IRA. The trust provides that in the event that Amy dies prior to the attainment of age 30, the trust remainderman is Sophie.

Assume that Janet dies on November 1, 2013, at age 74. Also assume that Janet received her entire required minimum distribution from her IRA for the calendar year 2013 before her date of death in the amount of $60,000.

The trustee of Janet's IRA trust satisfied the IRS post death trust documentation requirement with the IRA institution prior to the deadline of October 31, 2014. Amy attains age 12 in the calendar year 2014 and Sophie attains age 65 in the calendar year 2014.

Question: Over what term-certain period will the required minimum distributions be received from Janet's IRA by Janet's trust?

Answer: Janet's trust will receive required minimum distributions from Janet's IRA over a term-certain period of 21.0 years. This is based on the IRS single life expectancy of Sophie, not Amy, as determined in the calendar year after the year of death of Janet in 2013. In 2014, Sophie attains age 65. The IRS single life expectancy at age 65 is 21.0 years.

According to the IRS, if an individual trust beneficiary is not mandated the required minimum distributions each year, then all contingent beneficiaries determined as of Janet's date of death are considered in determining the designated beneficiary with the shortest life expectancy. As of the date of death of Janet, she was survived by both Amy and Sophie. Since Sophie is the oldest beneficiary, then her life expectancy is used because Amy was not the mandated trust beneficiary of the required minimum distributions under the terms of Janet's trust.

This approach was used in IRS letter ruling 200228025 dated April 18, 2002.

Situation 9

Assume the facts in Situation 8 except that Janet died on November 1, 2013, and received only $40,000 of her required minimum distribution of $60,000 for the calendar year 2013.

Question: Who receives the unpaid required minimum distribution of $20,000 for the calendar year 2013?

Answer: Janet's trust receives the unpaid required minimum distribution attributable to Janet for the calendar year 2013. See IRS final regulations at Section 1.401(a)(9)-5, A-4(a), which applies to plans and IRAs. That regulation provides that an unpaid required minimum distribution attributable to the deceased IRA owner's year of death must be distributed to a beneficiary to the extent that it has not been distributed to the IRA owner.

Situation 10

John, an IRA owner, creates a trust for the benefit of his son, Carl. The beneficiary of John's IRA is the John trust. The trust provides that Carl shall receive required minimum distributions from the trust until he attains age 40. In the event that Carl survives John and dies before the attainment of age 40, then the trust is payable to John's second son, Phil. Phil is five years older than Carl.

Assume that John dies on November 1, 2013. He would have attained age 76 on December 15, 2013, had he lived. Under the IRS rules, age 76 must be used in calculating John's lifetime required minimum distribution amount for the year of his death in 2013. Also assume that John received his entire required minimum distribution of $50,000 for the calendar year 2013 before his date of death. Carl attains age 30 in 2014 and Phil attains age 35 in 2014. Further assume that the trustee of John's trust failed to timely satisfy the IRS post death trust documentation requirement with the IRA institution by the October 31, 2014, deadline.

Question: May John's trust use the life expectancy of Carl or Phil in determining the distribution period that John's trust will use in determining required minimum distributions from John's IRA?

Answer: No. The failure to satisfy the IRS post death trust documentation requirement with the IRA institution by October 31, 2014, is a fatal defect. The deadline for this requirement is October 31 of the year following John's year of death in 2013. As a result, the life expectancy of a trust beneficiary cannot be used if the IRS post death trust documentation requirement is not timely satisfied with the IRA institution.

SITUATION **11**

Assume the facts in Situation 10.

Question: Over what term-certain period will the John trust receive required minimum distributions from John's IRA?

Answer: Since John died after his required beginning date, then John's trust uses a special IRS rule in determining required minimum distributions from John's IRA to John's trust. This special rule applies if an IRA owner dies on or after his or her required beginning date if a flunked trust or an estate is the beneficiary of an IRA. This special rule also applies if the IRA owner dies on or after his or her required beginning date and has an IRA beneficiary who is older than the IRA owner.

Based on the special rule, the John trust receives required minimum distributions commencing in 2014 over a term-certain period of 11.7 years. This is determined as follows:

(1) Determine the age John would have attained in the year of his death in 2013 had he not died. This is the starting point for the special IRS rule. In this case, he died on November 1, 2013, and would have attained age 76 on December 15, 2013, had he lived. According to the IRS rules, age 76 is the starting point.

(2) Then look at the IRS single life expectancy for an individual based on the attained age he or she would have been had he or she not died in the given year if the individual died on or after his or her required beginning date.

(3) The single life expectancy of an individual age 76 is 12.7 years, as determined in 2013. That number is reduced by one for each year thereafter. Accordingly, the John trust will receive required minimum distributions from John's IRA over an 11.7-year term-certain period commencing in the calendar year 2014. The 12.7 number is just the starting point and is not used for any other purpose. Remember that in 2013, John was alive as of January 1, 2013, and therefore computes his required minimum distribution for the calendar year 2013 under the lifetime rules. The special rule is used for determining

the term-certain period commencing in the calendar year 2014, the year after John's death.

Author's Note

If John had died before his required beginning date, then the five-year rule is applicable since his IRA beneficiary is a flunked trust. In that event, John's entire IRA account would have to be received by the John trust by no later than the end of the fifth year following the year of John's death.

SITUATION 12

Assume the facts in Situation 10 except that the trustee had timely satisfied the IRS post death trust documentation requirement by October 31, 2014.

Question: Over what term-certain period will John's trust receive required minimum distributions from John's IRA?

Answer: In that case, John's IRA trust is a qualifying IRA trust that can use the IRS single life expectancy of Carl, the primary individual trust beneficiary who survived John. Since Carl attains age 30 in 2014, then Carl's (not Phil's) IRS single life expectancy is used in determining the required minimum distributions to the John trust commencing in the calendar year 2014. The calendar year after the year of death of John is the year for the determination of Carl's IRS single life expectancy. The IRS single life expectancy of an individual age 30 in 2014 is 53.3 years. This number is used in 2014 and is reduced by one for each year thereafter.

Accordingly, the John trust in 2014 receives a required minimum distribution from John's IRA based in a term-certain number of 53.3 years. This amount is then paid by the trustee of John's trust to Carl. In 2015, for example, the number that is used in determining required minimum distribution to John's trust from John's IRA is 52.3. Once again, this number is reduced by one for each year thereafter.

> ## Author's Note
>
> A qualifying IRA trust is often referred to as a "conduit trust" or a "see-through" trust.
>
> According to the IRS rules, if the primary trust beneficiary, Carl, is mandated to receive the required minimum distributions under the terms of the trust, then the age of the contingent remainderman, Phil, is ignored.

* * *

> ## Author's Note
>
> In Situation 11, the term-certain period that is used in determining the required minimum distributions to John's flunked trust commencing in 2014 is 11.7 years. However, in Situation 12, the term-certain period that is used in determining the required minimum distributions to the John trust is 53.3 years.
>
> The difference of 41.6 years (53.3 − 11.7 = 41.6) is significant.

SITUATION 13

Assume that Paul, an IRA owner, had selected his estate as the beneficiary of his IRA. Under the terms of his will, any IRA payable to his estate will be used to fund a credit shelter trust under Article SEVENTH of his will. Further assume that the IRA is needed in order to fund the credit shelter trust.

Assume that the terms of the credit shelter trust mandate that the required minimum distributions received from Paul's IRA will be payable each year to his daughter, Julie. In addition, a copy of the trust provisions of Article SEVENTH of his will are timely sent to the IRA institution by the October 31 deadline after the year of Paul's death.

Question: Will the trustee of the Article SEVENTH trust under Paul's will receive required minimum distributions from Paul's IRA based on the IRS single life expectancy of Julie as determined in the calendar year after the year of Paul's death?

Answer: The IRS position is no. According to the IRS, an estate has no life expectancy. The fact that Paul's will provides that Paul's IRA will fund the trust under Article SEVENTH of Paul's will is not relevant.

Situation 14

Assume the facts in Situation 13 except that the beneficiary of Paul's IRA is the trust under Article SEVENTH of the last will and testament of Paul.

Question: Will the trustee of the Article SEVENTH trust under Paul's will receive required minimum distributions from Paul's IRA based on the IRS single life expectancy of Julie as determined in the calendar year after the year of Paul's death?

Answer: Yes. The IRS allows a trust beneficiary of a testamentary trust to be a designated beneficiary for life expectancy purposes if all the IRS rules are met.

DISCLOSURE ISSUES AND IRA TRUSTS

An IRA trust is a different type of trust that is not a form book type of trust.

It can be a separate trust that is dedicated to the receipt of distributions from an IRA, or it can be a trust under a will.

The separate trust that I recommend is created during the lifetime of the grantor and has all the terms that satisfy the IRS rules, including the IRS regulations and IRS letter rulings, and the state trust laws. In addition, the separate dedicated trust can be a dedicated revocable trust or a dedicated irrevocable trust. It is best to use a dedicated irrevocable trust for creditor rights protection purposes. An irrevocable trust is not an irrevocable beneficiary.

No matter what, the IRS post death trust documentation requirement must be timely satisfied with the IRA institution by no later than October 31 following the year of death of the IRA owner.

After the death of the IRA owner, the trustee must file annual fiduciary income tax returns with the IRS and the state if fiduciary income tax returns are required.

In the event that the IRA trust is not a qualifying IRA trust, then there may be significant problems for the trustee, trust beneficiary, trust attorney, and trust accountant.

The disclosure issues involving IRA trusts are best illustrated by the following example situations.

EXAMPLE

Scott, an IRA owner, creates a trust for the benefit of Martha, his daughter. He designates the Scott trust as the beneficiary of his IRA. Scott is advised that this trust can receive required minimum distributions from his IRA after his death based on the life expectancy of Martha as determined in the year after Scott's death. Murray is the trustee of the Scott trust.

The attorney drafts the trust, which provides that the Scott trust shall receive the required minimum distributions from Scott's IRA each year and that Martha shall receive the required minimum distributions from the trust each year. The trust further provides that if Martha dies before the attainment of age 60, the trust remainderman is the XYZ Charity.

Assume that Scott dies at age 79 in 2013 after receiving his required minimum distribution for the calendar year 2013.

In the calendar year 2014, the trustee receives a distribution from Scott's IRA in the amount of $20,000 based on Martha's IRS single life expectancy determined in the calendar year 2014. That amount is then paid to Martha. Harvey CPA prepares the fiduciary income tax return for the calendar year 2014, reporting the receipt of $20,000 as income for trust income tax purposes and deducting the $20,000 amount paid to Martha on the fiduciary income tax return as a distribution deduction.

For the calendar years 2015 and 2016, the process is continued, except that the amounts involved are $24,000 and $28,000, respectively.

In 2017, Harvey CPA takes a continuing education program on IRA issues and learns that Martha's IRS single life expectancy can be used by the trust only if the IRS post death trust documentation requirement was timely satisfied with the IRA institution by October 31, 2014.

After taking the continuing education program, Harvey calls Murray, the trustee, and asks him to send him the documentation that proves that Murray timely satisfied the IRS post death trust documentation requirement with the IRA institution by October 31, 2014.

Murray tells Harvey that he has no idea what Harvey is talking about. All that Murray knows is that the beneficiary form designated the trust as the beneficiary of Scott's IRA and that he was told by his financial adviser to use Martha's IRS single life expectancy as determined in the year after Scott's death in determining the annual required minimum distribution amount that must be made to the Scott trust each year.

It turns out that Murray never satisfied the IRS post death trust documentation requirement with the IRA institution by the October 31, 2014, deadline because no one told him about it.

Because of this noncompliance issue, the Scott trust erroneously received required minimum distributions from Scott's IRA under the IRS single life expectancy method that would otherwise be applicable to Martha had the error not been made.

Based on the oversight, Murray, as trustee of the Scott trust, must receive required minimum distributions from Scott's IRA over a 9.8-year term-certain period. This is based on a special IRS rule that applies if the IRA owner dies on or after his or her required beginning date under a certain set of circumstances, one of which is having a nonqualifying IRA trust as the beneficiary of an IRA.

Based on this error, the payments that Murray should have received from Scott's IRA each year based on Scott's 9.8-year term-certain period should have been in excess of $100,000 for each of the calendar years 2014, 2015, and 2016, respectively.

Murray is upset and afraid to do anything. He is worried about IRA penalties and having to give Martha significant sums of money over a relatively short-term period based on a 9.8-year term-certain period.

In addition, he is worried about litigation issues with Martha and Martha's remainderman. The trust remainderman is the XYZ Charity.

SITUATION 1

What should Harvey CPA do?

Answer: Treasury Department Circular No. 230 covers regulations governing practice before the Internal Revenue Service. See Sections 10.21 and 10.22.

Section 10.21, knowledge of client's omission, is on point. It states as follows:

> A practitioner who, having been retained by a client with respect to a matter administered by the Internal Revenue Service knows that the

client has not complied with the revenue laws of the United States or has made an error or omission from any return, document, affidavit or other paper which the client submitted or executed under the revenue laws of the United States, must advise the client promptly of the fact of such noncompliance, error or omission. The practitioner must advise the client of the consequences as provided under the Code and regulations of such noncompliance, error or omission.

Section 10.22 in Circular 230 covers diligence and states in part as follows:

1. In general a practitioner must exercise due diligence—In preparing or assisting in the preparation of approving and filing tax returns, documents, affidavits, and other papers relating to Internal Revenue Service matters; * * *

Harvey CPA should advise Murray to correct the situation going forward and to make up for the shortfall in required minimum distribution amounts as soon as possible. In addition, Harvey should recommend to Murray that Form 5329 be filed with the IRS for the years 2014, 2015, and 2016 indicating the shortfall amount and asking the IRS to waive the 50 percent excise tax for the calendar years 2014, 2015, and 2016 based on the technical issues involved in this case.

In order to request the IRS to grant a waiver of the 50 percent penalty, the taxpayer should indicate to the IRS that the shortfall amount was made up and in essence reported in the year when it was discovered and corrected. This means, for example, that the shortfall amount for 2014, 2015, and 2016 of over $300,000 plus the required minimum distribution amount for 2017 of over $100,000 should be received by the trustee of the Scott trust in 2017 and paid out to Martha, the trust beneficiary. Martha could have an additional $400,000-plus of trust income for the calendar year 2017 if Murray cooperates.

In the event that Murray refuses to cooperate, then Harvey CPA should point out to Murray that according to the 2011 Tax Court opinion in *Paschall v. Commissioner*, there is no statute of limitations on an IRA excise tax. That means that an IRS examiner can assert the 50 percent excise tax penalty on the shortfall amount in a required minimum distribution at any time since a Form 5329 was never filed with the IRS for the calendar years 2014, 2015, and 2016. Further, if a Form 5329 was never filed, then the IRS can assess delinquency filing penalties as well.

After all is said by Harvey CPA to Murray, if Murray still fails to act, then Harvey should consider resigning from the engagement to protect himself from problems with the IRS, the trust beneficiary, and the trust remainderman. In addition, Harvey may have to advise his malpractice carrier as to these issues. This may be required under the terms of his malpractice policy.

Author's Note

All of these headaches are triggered because of a simple slip-up on the failure to timely satisfy the IRS post death trust documentation requirement with the IRA financial institution.

It is surprising that the IRS has never issued a letter ruling that provides for an extension of the October 31 deadline. It is surely not the intention of the IRS to cause the problems described in this example. Perhaps a change in the Internal Revenue Code or IRS regulations is necessary to avoid the headaches described above.

SITUATION 2

Assume the facts in Situation 1. In addition, assume that Harvey CPA indicated to Murray that he has prepared many fiduciary income tax returns for the last 10 years and that one of the areas of concentration in his accounting practice is the preparation of fiduciary returns.

Question: Does Harvey face a malpractice liability suit based on the error made by Murray, the trustee?

Answer: Obviously, Murray may sue Harvey on the grounds that he represented that his practice included a concentration in the preparation of fiduciary income tax returns and that he should have advised Murray about the timely IRS post death trust documentation requirement.

Situation 3

Assume the same facts in Situation 1 and Situation 2, except that Harvey is an attorney (not a CPA) and concentrates in estate planning. In addition, he drafted the Scott trust and also prepares fiduciary income tax returns and estate tax returns. Further assume that Harvey, the attorney, did not tell Murray, the trustee, to timely satisfy the IRS post death trust documentation requirement with the IRA institution by the October 31 deadline because he did not know about it. He learned about the issue several years later.

Question: Does Harvey have an ethical obligation to inform his client, Murray, about this oversight after learning about it?

Answer: Yes. According to the American Bar Association Model Rules of Professional Conduct (Model Rules), the attorney has an obligation to communicate with his client, Murray, the trustee. The failure to communicate with a client and advise him or her as to the issue described above can result in an ethics problem for Harvey after he becomes aware of the problem. In addition, Harvey may have to notify his malpractice carrier about the issue as well. This may be required under the terms of his malpractice policy. Further, Harvey will probably have to withdraw as counsel to Murray since Murray has a potential malpractice claim against him.

In addition, an attorney under the Model Rules must satisfy an ethics rule of competence. If the attorney does not have the necessary knowledge in a subject area, then he or she can associate with or consult with an attorney that does have the necessary competence in the subject area. If Harvey does not know the IRA distribution rules (including IRS regulations, rulings, and notices), then he should consult with an attorney who does.

Alternatively, Harvey can become competent in the area by taking continuing education programs as well as obtaining other study material in the subject area. In addition, Harvey should keep on top of any changes in the IRS rules in the subject area.

Similar model rules of professional conduct have been adopted by many states.

APPLICATION OF THE UNIFORM PRINCIPAL AND INCOME ACT RULES IN NEW YORK STATE

The 1997 version of the model UPAIA has been adopted by over 40 states, with different effective dates.

New York State adopted a version of the act effective as of January 1, 2002, and has made changes from time to time.

In addition, New York State law permits both the power-of-adjustment and unitrust rules to be used. The unitrust provisions are not part of the UPAIA but are contained in separate provisions of the New York State trust law. Also, the power-to-adjust provisions are not part of the New York UPAIA but are contained in separate provisions of the New York State trust laws.

Each state's trust laws must be examined to determine the rules and effective dates of the rules that apply to trusts that are subject to the laws of that state.

The following are only a few examples of the trust accounting rules based on New York State trust law as it generally exists in 2013. Please note that periodic changes are made to the New York trust laws from time to time and may alter the suggested answers described in this book. The adviser to the trustee must read and analyze the trust laws that control the trust terms in a given state.

It should be noted that many states have adopted different versions of the 1997 UPAIA with different effective dates. In addition, many states have periodically changed their laws from time to time, with different effective dates as well.

The trust adviser has to keep up with the changes and advise the trustee as to the effective dates of the changes. This makes it difficult since the attorney who drafted the document years ago may no longer be in the picture today because of his or her death, retirement, or disability. This can be a problem for a trustee who assumes that the laws remain constant.

SOME EXAMPLES OF THE TRUST ACCOUNTING RULES IN NEW YORK STATE

POWER TO ADJUST

Situation 1

Assume that Jack dies on October 1, 2012. Jack's will establishes a trust for the benefit of his only daughter, Mary. Assume that Mary is divorced and earns only $15,000 a year as a part-time employee. The trust provides that Mary will receive the income from the trust each year. The remainderman of the trust is Cole, Mary's child. Harvey, Jack's former business associate, is the trustee. Harvey invests the trust assets primarily in equities. Further assume that during the calendar year 2013, the dividend and interest income that the trust will receive is approximately 1 percent of the fair market value of the trust assets as determined on January 2, 2013. This determination is made in November 2013. The fair market value of the trust assets as of January 2, 2013, amounts to approximately $1,000,000. Further assume that the unrealized capital gains for the calendar year appear to be approximately 5 percent of the fair market value of the trust assets as determined on January 2, 2013. This determination is also made in November 2013.

Question: Does Harvey, as trustee, have the power to adjust the income distribution to Mary from, for example, 1 percent to 3 percent so that Mary will receive a distribution of $30,000 ($1,000,000 × 3 percent) instead of $10,000 ($1,000,000 × 1 percent) from Jack's trust for the calendar year 2013?

Answer: Yes. According to EPTL 11-2.3(b)(5), where the rules in the UPAIA apply to a trust and the terms of the trust describe the amount that may or must be distributed to a beneficiary by referring to the trust's income, the prudent investor standard also authorizes the trustee to adjust between principal and income to the extent the trustee considers advisable based upon certain factors and accounting income expected to be produced by applying the rules under the New York UPAIA. Such adjustment would be deemed fair and reasonable to all the beneficiaries.

POWER TO ADJUST

Situation 2
Assume the facts in Situation 1.

Question: What in general does the prudent investor rule mean?

Answer: According to EPTL 11-2.3(b)(1), "the prudent investor rule requires a standard of conduct, not outcome or performance. Compliance with the prudent investor rule is determined in light of facts and circumstances prevailing at the time of the decision or action of a trustee. A trustee is not liable to a beneficiary to the extent that the trustee acted in substantial compliance with the prudent investor standard or in reasonable reliance on the express terms and provisions of the governing instrument."

Further, according to EPTL 11-2.3(b)(3)(A), "the prudent investor standard requires a trustee to pursue an overall investment strategy to enable the trustee to make appropriate present and future distributions to or for the benefit of the beneficiaries under the governing instrument, in accordance with risk and return objectives reasonably suited to the entire portfolio."

POWER TO ADJUST

Situation 3
Assume the facts in Situation 2.

Question: What factors should Harvey, as trustee, consider in determining whether or not to exercise the power to adjust?

Answer: According to EPTL 11-2.3, a trustee may consider a number of factors, including the following:

(1) The nature and estimated duration of the fiduciary relationship.

(2) The liquidity and distribution requirements of the governing instrument.

(3) The expected tax consequences of investment decisions or strategies and of distributions of income and principal.

(4) The expected total return of the portfolio (including both income and appreciation of capital).

(5) The needs of beneficiaries (to the extent reasonably known to the trustee) for present and future distributions authorized or required by the governing instrument.

(6) To consider related trusts, the income and resources of beneficiaries to the extent reasonably known to the trustee.

(7) The intent of the settlor, as expressed in the governing instrument.

(8) The net amount allocated to income under [the UPAIA] and the increase or decrease in the value of the principal assets, which the trustee may estimate as to assets for which market values are not readily available.

(9) Whether and to what extent the terms of the trust give the trustee the power to invade principal or accumulate income or prohibit the trustee from invading principal or accumulating income, and the extent to which the trustee has exercised a power from time to time to invade principal or accumulate income.

(10) The trustee may consider the accounting income expected to be produced by applying the rules under the New York Uniform Principal and Income Act and that such adjustment would be fair and reasonable to all the beneficiaries.

POWER TO ADJUST

Situation 4

Assume that John dies on November 1, 2012. In his will, John created a trust for the benefit of his daughter, Jane. The trust is funded on January 2, 2013. It is required to pay the income from the trust to Jane each year. In addition, Carl, the trustee, may invade principal to benefit Jane's health, education, maintenance, and support. Further assume that the trustee determines in November 2013 that the interest and dividend income for the calendar year 2013 is anticipated to be approximately 2 percent of the value of the principal of the trust as determined on January 2, 2013.

Question: May Carl, the trustee of John's trust, exercise the power to adjust on behalf of Jane for the calendar year 2013?

Answer: Yes. The Fifth Report of the EPTL-SCPA Legislative Advisory Committee, May 11, 1999, at Example 3 provides some guidance on this issue.

Example (3): T is the trustee of a trust that requires the income to be paid to the settlor's sister E for life, remainder to charity F. E is a retired school teacher who is single and has no children. E's income from her social security, pension, and savings exceeds the amount required to provide for her accustomed standard of living. The terms of the trust permit T to invade principal to provide for E's health and to support her in her accustomed manner of living, but do not otherwise indicate that T should favor E or F. Applying the prudent investor rule, T determines that the trust assets should be invested entirely in growth stocks that produce very little dividend income. Even though it is not necessary to invade principal to maintain E's accustomed standard of living, she is entitled to receive from the trust the degree of beneficial enjoyment normally accorded a person who is the sole income beneficiary of a trust, and T may transfer cash from principal to income to provide her with that degree of enjoyment.

POWER TO ADJUST

Situation 5

Assume the facts in Situation 4. Also assume that Carl, the trustee, is the remainderman of John's trust.

Question: Under these circumstances, may Carl exercise the power to adjust on behalf of Jane for the calendar year 2013?

Answer: No. According to EPTL 11-2.3(b)(5)(C)(vii), a trustee may not make an adjustment if he or she is a current beneficiary or a presumptive remainderman of the trust unless there is express provision in the trust that permits such trustee to make the adjustment. However, under EPTL 11-2.3(b)(5)(D), the court may permit the adjustment upon the application of the trustee or an interested party if there is no trustee qualified to make the adjustment.

Author's Note

According to EPTL 11-2.3(b)(5)(D), if there is more than one trustee, a cotrustee to whom the provision does not apply may make the adjustment unless the exercise of the power by the remaining trustee or trustees is not permitted by the terms of the trust.

POWER TO ADJUST

Situation 6

Assume that Marvin has a significant IRA that is payable to a trust for the benefit of his daughter, Karen. Marvin, age 68, dies on December 1, 2013. Harry, as trustee, timely satisfies the documentation requirements of the Internal Revenue Service with the IRA institution by no later than the October 31, 2014, deadline. Karen is the income beneficiary of the trust. The remainderman of the trust is Judy, Marvin's niece, who is younger than Karen. Further assume that the value of Marvin's IRA that is payable to Marvin's trust is $1,000,000 as of December 31, 2013. The required minimum distribution that must be made to the trust from Marvin's IRA for the calendar year 2014 is $30,000. Assume that the trust has no other earnings for the calendar year 2014.

Question: What is the amount of the income distribution that must be made to Karen from Marvin's trust for the calendar year 2014?

Answer: According to EPTL 11-A-4.9(c), only 10 percent of the required minimum distribution must be paid to Karen as an income distribution for the calendar year 2014. Therefore, only $3,000 ($30,000 × 10 percent) will be distributed to Karen as an income distribution for the calendar year 2014.

POWER TO ADJUST

Situation 7

Assume the facts in Situation 6. Further assume that Harry, as trustee, distributes $30,000 to Karen instead of $3,000 for the calendar year 2014. The reason for the excess distribution to Karen is that Harry did not know the difference between accounting income as determined under the state law (UPAIA) and taxable income as determined under the federal law.

Question: What options are available to Harry as trustee?

Answer: Harry, as trustee, has several options.

(1) Requesting that Karen return the extra $27,000 to Marvin's trust on a voluntary basis

(2) Obtaining a release from the remainderman as to the excess distribution to Karen

(3) Withholding future distributions from Karen to make up for the overpayment

(4) Commencing an action against Karen in the surrogate's court that has jurisdiction over Marvin's trust to recover the $27,000 overpayment

POWER TO ADJUST

Situation 8

Assume the facts in Situation 6. Further assume that Harry, as trustee of Marvin's trust, overpaid Karen for many years and that the total over-payments to Karen amount to $350,000. Also assume that Karen has no money since she paid income taxes on these distributions and spent all her money on living expenses.

Question: What happens to Harry under these circumstances?

Answer: Harry, as trustee, will have to settle with Judy, the remainder-man, on some reasonable basis. If no settlement is reached, then Judy can bring an action for an accounting in the Surrogate's Court that has juris-diction over Marvin's trust. Obviously, Harry has a significant problem and faces massive monetary liabilities.

POWER TO ADJUST

Situation 9

Assume the facts in Situation 8. Further assume that Donald, the profes-sional adviser to the trustee, prepared trust fiduciary income tax returns of Marvin's trust for the calendar year 2014 and for many years thereafter. Donald did not know the difference between accounting income under the state law and taxable income as determined under the federal law for all the years that he prepared the trust fiduciary income tax returns for Marvin's trust. Donald is an enrolled agent who prepares many tax returns, including fiduciary income tax returns, each year.

Question: What problems does Donald face?

Answer: Donald may have major liability problems. He faces lawsuits from Harry, the trustee; Karen, the income beneficiary; and Judy, the remainderman. In the event of any liability regarding his professional activities involving the trust, his malpractice liability insurance policy may protect him from any significant exposure. The lawsuit against Donald would be based upon his lack of knowledge about the state trust laws. The theory of the liability against Donald would then be as follows:

(1) He may have held himself out as an expert to Harry, the trustee.

(2) If he did, then he should have known about the state trust law rules.

(3) Harry, the trustee, relied upon Donald with respect to administering Marvin's trust.

(4) Donald was given a copy of Marvin's trust document by Harry, the trustee, and was asked to review the provisions of the trust document.

POWER TO ADJUST

Situation 10

Assume the facts in Situation 9.

Question: What possible defenses to the lawsuit does Donald have?

Answer: Donald's retainer agreement may protect him. The retainer agreement with Harry, the trustee of Marvin's trust, may provide as follows:

(1) Donald is engaged solely to prepare the trust's fiduciary income tax return.

(2) In connection with the tax compliance function with respect to Marvin's trust, Donald is to rely solely on the financial information given to him by Harry, the trustee, in order to prepare the trust's fiduciary income tax returns.

(3) Donald is not responsible to Harry, the trustee, for the interpretation of the trust document and/or the New York State trust laws.

(4) Harry, the trustee, will be responsible for the matters mentioned in item 3.

(5) Harry, the trustee, acknowledges that Donald has advised him to seek independent counsel with respect to the matters mentioned in item 3.

(6) Harry, the trustee, releases Donald from any and all liability that may arise with respect to the matters mentioned in item 3.

POWER TO ADJUST

Situation 11

Assume the facts in Situation 7. Further assume that Donald becomes aware of the 2014 erroneous overpayment of $27,000 to Karen during 2015. He learns about the 10 percent income rule by reading about it in a business journal that he subscribes to.

Question: What should Donald do?

Answer: Donald should immediately notify Harry, the trustee, as to the erroneous 2014 overpayment to Karen. This is not only the smart thing to do; it is the right thing to do. Ethically, Donald should take the high road and take his chances from a malpractice point of view. If Donald ignores the issue after he knows about it, then he is risking a formal ethics charge against him at a later date as well as increased malpractice exposure. Harry, as the trustee, may accept Donald's excuse and not discharge him. Donald should present the information to Harry in a diplomatic manner. This discussion should include the fact that very few professionals are aware of the 10 percent UPAIA income rule regarding required minimum distributions that are paid to a trust. He should also show Harry a copy of the law. The law does not read like a novel.

POWER TO ADJUST

Situation 12

Assume that Tom has a significant IRA that is payable to a trust for the benefit of his son, Harvey. Tom, age 67, dies on October 1, 2013. Murray, as trustee, timely satisfies the documentation requirements of the IRS with the IRA institution by no later than the October 31, 2014, deadline. Harvey is the income beneficiary of the trust. The remainderman of the trust is Mary, a niece who is younger than Harvey. The value of Tom's IRA that is payable to Tom's trust is $800,000 as of December 31, 2013. The required minimum distribution that must be made to the trust from Tom's IRA for the calendar year 2014 is $35,000. Assume that the trust has no other earnings for the calendar year 2014.

Question: What is the amount of the income distribution that must be made to Harvey for the calendar year 2014?

Answer: According to EPTL 11-A-4.9(c), only 10 percent of the required minimum distribution must be paid to Harvey as an income distribution for the calendar year 2014. Therefore, only $3,500 (10 percent of $35,000) will be distributed to Harvey as an income distribution for the calendar year 2014.

POWER TO ADJUST

Situation 13

Assume the facts in Situation 12.

Question: May Murray, as trustee, increase the income distribution from Tom's trust to Harvey from, for example, $3,500 to $27,500 for the calendar year 2014?

Answer: Yes. At his discretion, Murray, as trustee, has the power to increase the income distribution to Harvey, the trust beneficiary, from $3,500 to $27,500 for the calendar year 2014.

The Fifth Report of the EPTL-SCPA Legislative Advisory Committee, May 11, 1999, at Example 5 provides some guidance on the issue.

> Example (5): T is the trustee for the settlor's child. The trust owns a diversified portfolio of marketable financial assets with a value of $600,000 and is also the sole beneficiary of the settlor's IRA, which holds a diversified portfolio of marketable financial assets with a value of $900,000. The trust receives a distribution from the IRA that is the minimum amount required to be distributed under the Internal Revenue Code, and T allocates 10% of the distribution to income under Section 11-A-4.9(c). The total return on the IRA's assets exceeds the amount distributed to the trust, and the value of the IRA at the end of the year is more than its value at the beginning of the year. Relevant factors that T may consider in determining whether to exercise the power to adjust and the extent to which an adjustment should be made to comply with Section

11-A-1.3(b) include the total return from all of the trust's assets, those owned directly as well as its interest in the IRA, the extent to which the trust will be subject to income tax on the portion of the IRA distribution that is allocated to principal, and the extent to which the income beneficiary will be subject to income tax on the amount that T distributes to the income beneficiary.

POWER TO ADJUST

Situation 14

Assume the facts in Situation 13.

Question: Before a trustee may exercise a power to adjust, must he or she first consider the adjustments that are applicable or permissible under the UPAIA?

Answer: Yes. According to EPTL 11-2.3(b)(5)(A), if the UPAIA applies to a trust and the trust refers to permissive or mandatory income distributions to a beneficiary, then the trustee has the power to adjust after applying the rules in the UPAIA.

EPTL 11-A-1.3(b) [of the UPAIA] provides in part that in exercising a discretionary power of administration [under the UPAIA], a fiduciary must administer a trust . . . impartially, based on what is fair and reasonable to all of the beneficiaries, except to the extent that the terms of the trust . . . clearly manifest an intention that the fiduciary shall or may favor one or more of the beneficiaries. A determination in accordance with [the UPAIA] is presumed to be fair and reasonable to all of the beneficiaries.

POWER TO ADJUST

Situation 15

Assume that Jack is the trustee of a trust for the benefit of Charles, the income beneficiary of the trust. During the calendar year 2013, Jack, as trustee, determines not to exercise the power to adjust in favor of Charles because he feels that Charles has sufficient outside independent income.

Question: Who is likely to prevail in the event that Charles brings a lawsuit against Jack for his decision not to exercise the power of adjustment in favor of Charles?

Answer: Perhaps Jack, the trustee. According to EPTL 11-2.3-A(a), "a court [will] not challenge a fiduciary's decision to exercise or not to exercise an adjustment power conferred [under EPTL 11-2.3(b)(5)] unless it determines that the decision was an abuse of the fiduciary's discretion. A court [will] not determine that a fiduciary abused his, her or its discretion merely because the court would have exercised the discretion in a different manner or would not have exercised the discretion."

POWER TO ADJUST

Situation 16

Assume the facts in Situation 15.

Question: In the absence of an abuse of discretion, what fiduciary decisions will the court generally not reverse?

Answer: According to EPTL 11-2.3-A(b), the fiduciary's decisions that the court generally will not change include the following:

1. A determination under [the power to adjust] of whether and to what extent an amount should be transferred from principal to income or from income to principal.

2. A determination of the factors that are relevant to the trust and its beneficiaries, the extent to which they are relevant, and the weight, if any, to be given to the relevant factors, in deciding whether and to what extent to exercise the power [to adjust].

POWER TO ADJUST

Situation 17

Assume the facts in Situation 15.

Question: If Jack, as trustee, is concerned about his decision not to exercise the power to adjust in favor of Charles, the income beneficiary, what action can Jack take to protect himself?

Answer: Jack, as trustee, can request the court to back his decision not to exercise the power to adjust in favor of Charles. According to EPTL 11-2.3-A(d),

> upon a petition by a fiduciary who is authorized to exercise an adjustment power [under EPTL 11-2.3(b)(5)], the court having jurisdiction over the trust . . . may determine whether a proposed exercise or nonexercise by the fiduciary of the adjustment power will result in an abuse of the fiduciary's discretion. If the petition describes the proposed exercise or nonexercise of the power and contains sufficient information to inform the beneficiaries of the reasons for the proposal, the facts upon which the fiduciary relies, and an explanation of how the income and remainder beneficiaries will be affected by the proposed exercise or nonexercise of the power, a beneficiary who challenges the proposed exercise or nonexercise has the burden of establishing that it will result in an abuse of discretion.

POWER TO ADJUST

Situation 18

Assume that Marvin, a trustee of a trust for the benefit of Mary, the income beneficiary of the trust, improperly failed to exercise his power to adjust in favor of Mary. Assume that Mary, as beneficiary, petitions the court for relief.

Question: What action can the court take?

Answer: According to EPTL 11-2.3-A(c),

> if a court determines that a fiduciary has abused his, her or its discretion regarding the power to adjust, the court may restore the income and remainder beneficiaries to the positions they would

have occupied if the fiduciary had not abused his, her or its discretion, according to the following rules:

1. To the extent that the abuse of discretion has resulted in no distribution to a beneficiary or a distribution that is too small, the court shall require the fiduciary to distribute from the trust to the beneficiary an amount that the court determines will restore the beneficiary, in whole or in part, to his or her appropriate position.

2. To the extent that the abuse of discretion has resulted in a distribution to a beneficiary that is too large, the court shall restore the beneficiaries, the trust, or both, in whole or in part, to their appropriate positions by requiring the fiduciary to withhold an amount from one or more future distributions to the beneficiary who received the distribution that was too large or requiring that beneficiary to return some or all of the distribution to the trust.

3. To the extent that the court is unable after applying [(1) and (2)], to restore the beneficiaries, the trust, or both to the positions they would have occupied if the fiduciary had not abused his, her or its discretion, and if the court finds that the fiduciary was dishonest or arbitrary and capricious in the exercise of his, her or its discretion, the court may require the fiduciary to pay an appropriate amount from his, her or its own funds to one or more of the beneficiaries or the trust or both.

POWER TO ADJUST

Situation 19

Assume that Frank dies on October 1, 2012, leaving a trust for the benefit of his only child, Harry. The terms of the trust provide that Harry shall receive income from the trust each year. The remainderman of the trust is Harry's child, Donald (Frank's grandchild). Further assume that Morris, the trustee, has the absolute discretion to invade the principal of the trust on behalf of Harry at any time for Harry's health, education, maintenance, and support. Morris is a former business associate of Frank. He invests primarily in equities. As of January 2, 2013, the fair market value of the assets in the trust is $1,000,000. The interest income and dividend income of the trust assets for the calendar year 2013 is projected to be 1 percent of the fair market value of the trust assets as determined on January 2, 2013. This means that Harry will receive only approximately $10,000 as the income beneficiary of Frank's trust for the calendar year 2013. The projected increase in equities for the calendar year 2013 appears to be in excess of 5 percent of the fair value of the trust assets as determined on January 2, 2013. The projections as to income and equities increases are made on October 31, 2013. Further assume that Harry on November 15, 2013, requests that Morris invade principal on his behalf because he feels that the income earned by the trust is insufficient. Morris states to Harry, the income beneficiary, that he does not wish to exercise this discretion regarding the invasion of principal because he does not feel that Harry needs the money. Nothing is said about Morris's ability to exercise a power to adjust because both Morris and Harry are not aware of the law that gives him that power. Assume that in 2014, Harry finds out that Morris, as trustee, had the legal authority to exercise a power to adjust and transfer funds from principal to income for Harry's benefit for the year 2013.

Question: Should Harry, the income beneficiary, commence a proceeding against Morris, the trustee, for an additional income distribution of $20,000 from the trust for the calendar year 2013 on the grounds that Morris, as trustee, failed to make a decision, one way or another, regarding whether or not to exercise his discretion with respect to the power to adjust?

Answer: Yes. The court could probably make an independent decision as to whether or not the power to adjust in favor of Harry should be made. It would appear that the court would not have to examine whether or not Morris, the trustee, abused his discretion regarding a decision to exercise or not to exercise the power to adjust. Since Morris, as trustee, did not know about his power to adjust, he could not have made a decision regarding whether or not to exercise his power to adjust.

POWER TO ADJUST

Situation 20

Assume that Phillip wishes to establish an estate plan for himself during the calendar year 2013. His estate plan will include trusts for his children and grandchildren. He is also informed during 2013 about the revised trust laws in New York State. His best friend, Mark, will be his trustee. Phillip does not wish to burden Mark with the power-to-adjust rules under the revised trust laws under New York State law.

Question: May Phillip opt out of the power-to-adjust rules in his trust document?

Answer: Yes. According to EPTL 11-2.3(b)(5)(F), "the terms of a trust that limit the power of a trustee to make an adjustment between principal and income are not contrary to [the power-to-adjust rules] unless it is clear from the terms of the trust that the terms are intended to deny the trustee the power of adjustment conferred by [EPTL 11-2.3(b)(5)(A)]."

UNITRUST

Situation 21

New York State law as of January 1, 2002, permits a trust to operate as a unitrust.

Question: Why is the optional unitrust provision important?

Answer: If the unitrust rules are applicable, then the trustee is required to determine the amount of the net income that is to be distributed to an income beneficiary based upon a percentage of the net fair market value of the trust assets. It eliminates the need for the trustee to apply the rules under the UPAIA and to exercise the power to adjust. In the event that a trust is subject to the optional unitrust provision under EPTL 11-2.4, then the UPAIA and the power-to-adjust rules do not apply to the trust. The optional unitrust provision applies to a trust that provides for income distributions to a beneficiary. A trust can be drafted in a manner that precludes the use of the unitrust rules or that specifically requires their use. In the event that the trust refers to net income and is otherwise silent about the unitrust rules, then the trustee or beneficiary can take certain actions either together or separately with respect to the implementation of the unitrust rules.

UNITRUST

Situation 22

New York State trust law permits a trust to operate as a unitrust under certain circumstances.

Question: When does a trust become subject to the unitrust rules?

Answer: According to EPTL 11-2.4(e)(1), the unitrust rules (the optional unitrust provision) apply to a trust under the following circumstances:

1. The governing instrument provides that the unitrust rules [EPTL 11-2.4] will apply to the trust, or

2. With respect to a trust in existence prior to January 1, 2002, on or before December 31, 2005, the trustee with the consent by or on behalf of all persons interested in the trust or in his, her or its discretion, elects to have the [optional unitrust provisions] under EPTL 11-2.4 apply to the trust, or

3. With respect to a trust not in existence prior to January 1, 2002, on or before the last day of the second full year of the trust beginning after assets first become subject to the trust, the trustee with the consent by or on behalf of all persons interested in the trust or in his, her or its discretion, elects to have [the optional unitrust provision] under EPTL 11-2.4 apply to the trust.

UNITRUST

Situation 23

Assume that Harold dies on November 1, 2012. Harold's will establishes a trust for the benefit of his daughter, Diane. The trust provides that Diane shall receive the income from the trust each year, and on her death, the remainder shall be paid to Craig, Harold's grandchild. The trustee of the trust is Norman. The trust assets are transferred to the trust on March 1, 2013.

Question: When do the trust assets become subject to Harold's trust under the unitrust rules?

Answer: According to EPTL 11-2.4(d)(1)(B), the trust assets would become subject to Harold's trust on the date it is transferred to the trust in the case of an asset that is transferred to a testamentary trust created under a will. In this case, the assets first become subject to Harold's trust on March 1, 2013.

UNITRUST

Situation 24
Assume the facts in Situation 23. Also assume that Norman, the trustee, wishes to elect that the unitrust rules shall apply to Harold's trust.

Question: By what date may Norman, as trustee, elect that the unitrust rules apply to the trust?

Answer: According to EPTL 11-2.4(e)(1)(B)(ii), since the trust was not in existence prior to January 1, 2002, he must elect to have the unitrust rules (the optional unitrust provision) apply to Harold's trust by no later than the last day of the second full year of the trust beginning after assets first become subject to the trust. In this case, the assets first become subject to the trust on March 1, 2013. Accordingly, the last day of the second full year of the trust after March 1, 2013, is December 31, 2015.

UNITRUST

Situation 25
Assume the facts in Situation 24. Further assume that Norman, as trustee, would like to elect that the unitrust rules (the optional unitrust provision) apply to Harold's trust as of January 1, 2014.

Question: What steps should Norman, as a trustee, take and when?

Answer: Norman, as trustee, could elect by no later than December 31, 2013, that the optional unitrust provision under EPTL 11-2.4 applies to Harold's trust effective as of January 1, 2014. The authority for the selection of this effective date is found in EPTL 11-2.4(e)(4)(A).

According to EPTL 11-2.4(e)(1)(B)(iii), an election is made by the trustee by an instrument executed, acknowledged, and delivered by the creator of the trust, if he or she is then living, to all persons interested in the trust or to their representatives and to the court, if any, having jurisdiction over the trust.

Author's Note

The election method is probably easier than having to obtain the written consent of or on behalf of all persons interested in the trust.

In addition, an election by Norman, the trustee, could be made during the calendar year 2014 that the unitrust provisions apply as of January 1, 2014, as well.

UNITRUST

Situation 26

Assume the facts in Situation 24 except that Norman, the trustee, would like to elect that the unitrust rules (the optional unitrust provision) apply to Harold's trust as of March 1, 2013.

Question: May Norman, as trustee, elect that the unitrust rules apply to the trust as of March 1, 2013?

Answer: Yes. According to EPTL 11-2.4(e)(4)(A), Norman, as trustee, may prior to December 31, 2013, elect that the unitrust rules (optional unitrust provision) apply to Harold's trust as of the first year of the trust in which assets first become subject to the trust unless his (timely) election is expressly made effective as of the first day of the first year of the trust commencing after the election is made.

Author's Note

According to EPTL 11-2.4(b)(6), in the case of a short year, the trustee must prorate the unitrust amount on a daily basis.

UNITRUST

Situation 27

Assume the facts in Situation 24 except that Norman, the trustee, would like to elect that the unitrust rules (optional unitrust provision) apply to the trust as of January 1, 2015.

Question: What steps should Norman, as trustee, take and when?

Answer: Norman, as trustee, could make an election during the calendar year 2015 to the effect that the optional unitrust provision under EPTL 11-2.4 applies to this trust effective as of January 1, 2015. The authority for the selection of this effective date is found in EPTL 11-2.4(e)(4)(A).

Author's Note

Under the current law, there is authority under EPTL 11-2.4(e)(4)(A) for Norman, as trustee, to select an effective date of January 1, 2015, if he makes an election in the calendar year 2015.

In addition, if Norman, the trustee, would like to have the unitrust rules apply to the trust as of January 1, 2015, he could make the election during the calendar year 2014 to have the unitrust provisions apply as of January 1, 2015.

UNITRUST

Situation 28

Assume that Mark dies on October 1, 2012. His will establishes a trust for the benefit of Mary, his daughter. The trust provides that Mary shall receive the income from the trust each year. Karen, Mark's grandchild, is the remainderman. The assets are transferred to the trust on July 1, 2013. During 2014, Carl, the trustee, elects that the unitrust rules (the optional unitrust provision) apply to the trust as of January 1, 2014.

Question: What is the effect of the unitrust election with respect to Mary's distributions from the trust?

Answer: According to EPTL 11-2.4(a), unless the terms of the trust provide otherwise, the net income of the trust shall mean the unitrust amount as determined under the unitrust rules. Therefore, Mary's income distributions from Mark's trust for the calendar year 2014 are the unitrust amount.

UNITRUST

Situation 29

Assume the facts in Situation 28. Also assume that the net fair market value of the trust assets amount to $1,000,000 as of January 2, 2014. Further assume that the unitrust rules (the optional unitrust provision) are applicable as of January 1, 2014.

Question: How much is the unitrust amount that must be received by Mary for the calendar year 2014?

Answer: $40,000. According to EPTL 11-2.4(b)(1), the unitrust amount for the first three years of the trust as a unitrust shall mean an amount equal to 4 percent of the net fair market values of the assets held in the trust on the first business day of the current valuation year. According to EPTL 11-2.4(c)(5), the net fair market value (generally) means the fair market value of each asset comprising the trust reduced by any outstanding interest-bearing obligations of the trust, whether allocable to a specific asset or otherwise.

Author's Note

According to EPTL 11-2.4(c)(4), "the term 'year' means a calendar year."

UNITRUST

Situation 30

Assume the facts in Situation 29. Further assume that Mary dies on July 1, 2014. Further assume that during 2014, Mary received a partial distribution of $5,000 from Mark's trust prior to her death.

Question: How much is Mary's estate entitled to receive from Mark's trust for the calendar year 2014?

Answer: $15,000. Mary's income interest came to an end on June 30, 2014, the day before death, according to the UPAIA. According to EPTL 11-2.4(b)(6), in the case of a short year, the trustee must prorate the unitrust amount on a daily basis. Therefore, the unitrust amount for one-half of a year is $20,000 ($40,000 × 50 percent). Since Mary received $5,000 of the unitrust amount prior to her death, then the remaining balance of the unitrust amount of $15,000 for half a year is payable to her estate. According to EPTL 11-2.4(c)(4), "the term 'year' means a calendar year. A short year constitutes a portion of a calendar year that begins when the interest of the current beneficiary . . . begins or ends when the interest of the current beneficiary . . . ends."

UNITRUST

Situation 31

Harry establishes a revocable trust for the benefit of Martin, his son, on July 1, 2012, and funds the revocable trust on that date. The terms of the revocable trust provide that Martin is to receive the income from the trust each year after the death of Harry. The trust remainderman is Jack, Harry's nephew. Assume that Harry dies on October 1, 2013. Further assume that on November 1, 2013, Martin requests that Tom, the trustee, elect that the unitrust rules (the optional unitrust provision) apply to Harry's trust at the earliest possible date under the law.

Question: What is the earliest date that the unitrust rules (the optional unitrust provision) may apply to Harry's trust?

Answer: October 1, 2013. According to EPTL 11-2.4(e)(4)(A) and under these circumstances, it is possible to have the unitrust rules apply as of the first year of the trust in which assets first become subject to the trust. According to EPTL 2.4(d)(1)(E), an asset becomes subject to a trust "on the date a revocable trust becomes irrevocable in the case of assets then held in the trust."

Author's Note

The year 2013 is a short year since Harry's date of death is October 1, 2013.

UNITRUST

Situation 32

Assume the facts in Situation 31. Further assume that Tom, the trustee, ignores Martin's request to elect that the unitrust rules (the optional unitrust provision) apply to the trust.

Question: What option is available to Martin?

Answer: Martin can petition the court that the unitrust rules (the optional unitrust provision) apply to the trust. According to EPTL 11-2.4(e)(2)(B), "at any time, the court having jurisdiction of a trust . . . upon the petition of the trustee or any beneficiary of the trust and upon notice to all persons interested in the trust, may direct that [the optional unitrust provision] shall apply to the trust and that [the UPAIA] shall not apply to the trust." According to EPTL 11-2.4(e)(4)(A), the court in its decision can direct that the unitrust rules, and the optional unitrust provision, shall be effective as of the first year of the trust in which assets first become subject to the trust (in this case, 2013) unless the court in its decision provides otherwise.

Author's Note

The year 2013 is a short year since Harry's date of death is October 1, 2013.

UNITRUST

Situation 33

Assume the facts in Situation 32.

Question: Does Martin have a reasonable probability of success in his petition to the court to have a decision in his favor on the unitrust issue?

Answer: Yes. According to EPTL 11-2.4(e)(5)(B), in any court proceeding brought pursuant to the petition of the trustee or any beneficiary of the trust, there shall be a rebuttable presumption that the unitrust optional provision should apply to the trust.

Author's Note

The rebuttable presumption language means that the odds of success are in Martin's favor in having the court render a decision that directs that the unitrust provisions apply to Harry's trust.

UNITRUST

Situation 34

Assume that Harold is the income beneficiary of a trust. The net fair market value of the trust assets is $1,000,000 as of January 2, 2013. Assume that the unitrust rules are applicable for the calendar year 2013. Assume that the calendar year 2013 is the first year of the unitrust. During the calendar year 2013, the expenses of the trust amount to $5,000.

Question: How much does Harold receive from the trust for the calendar year 2013?

Answer: $40,000. The unitrust amount for the current valuation year 2013 is equal to 4 percent of the net fair market value of the assets held in the trust on the first business day of the current valuation year. The expenses of $5,000 are not charged against the unitrust amount.

UNITRUST

Situation 35

Assume the facts in Situation 34. Also assume that the trust received dividend income of $12,000 and interest income of $3,000 for the calendar year 2013. In addition, the trust incurred $5,000 of expenses for the calendar year 2013.

Question: With respect to the $40,000 unitrust amount that is paid to Harold, how much of that amount is taxable to him on his Form 1040 for the calendar year 2013?

Answer: $10,000. The net ordinary income of the trust is computed as follows:

Dividend income	$12,000
Interest income	3,000
Gross income	$15,000
Less: Expenses	5,000
Net ordinary income	$10,000

Author's Note

Harold receives $40,000 as the unitrust amount for the calendar year 2013 but needs to report only $10,000. The $30,000 ($40,000 – $10,000) difference between the unitrust amount and the net ordinary income of the trust is tax-free to Harold.

UNITRUST

Situation 36

Assume that Harvey is the income beneficiary of a trust that was in existence on March 1, 2000. Further assume that Jack, the trustee of the trust, failed to elect the unitrust rules (the optional unitrust provision) by December 31, 2005.

Question: During the calendar year 2014, may Jack or Harvey petition the court that the unitrust rules (the optional unitrust provision) apply to the trust as of January 1, 2014?

Answer: Yes. According to EPTL 11-2.4(e)(2)(B), at any time, the court having jurisdiction of a trust, upon the petition of the trustee or any beneficiary of the trust and upon notice to all persons interested in the trust, direct that the optional unitrust provision shall apply to the trust and that the UPAIA shall not apply to the trust.

UNITRUST

Situation 37

Assume that Steve is the income beneficiary of Carl's trust. Further assume that the trust is not subject to the unitrust rules with respect to Steve. Steve dies on October 1, 2013. On Steve's death, the assets in Carl's trust are held in further trust for the benefit of Jack. Jack is the income beneficiary of this trust. Howard is the trustee of both trusts.

Question: May Howard elect that the unitrust rules (the optional unitrust provision) apply to the trust for the benefit of Jack?

Answer: Yes. According to EPTL 11-2.4(d)(2), a trust which continues in existence for the benefit of one or more new current beneficiaries or classes of current beneficiaries, upon the termination of the interests of all prior current beneficiaries or class of prior current beneficiaries shall be deemed to be a new trust. For purposes of applying the unitrust rules, assets shall first become subject to the trust on the date of the termination of such prior interest.

UNITRUST

Situation 38

Assume the facts in Situation 37.

Question: May Howard, as the trustee, elect during 2014 that the unitrust rules (the optional unitrust provision) apply to the trust for the benefit of Jack as of January 1, 2014?

Answer: Yes. Based upon EPTL 11-2.4(d)(2), the trust for the benefit of Jack is deemed to be a new trust. Since the assets become subject to the new trust for purposes of the unitrust election rules as of October 1, 2013, Howard, as trustee, may elect during 2013 or 2014 that the trust for the benefit of Jack shall become subject to the unitrust rules (the optional unitrust provision) as of January 1, 2014. In addition, all the unitrust consent and election rules that apply to a trust as if it were in existence prior to January 1, 2002, are applicable to the trust for the benefit of Jack.

Author's Note

I take a position that the new interest for purposes of the unitrust election commences on October 1, 2013. However, technically and according to the UPAIA, the prior interest ends the day before death, which is September 30, 2013. According to unitrust provisions, the new interest starts on the date that the prior interest ends, which would also be September 30, 2013. However, I believe that the unitrust statute should have stated that the new trust for unitrust purposes starts the day after the prior interest ends. That is the approach used under the UPAIA. That is why I chose October 1, 2013, as the answer.

DISTRIBUTABLE NET INCOME

Situation 39

Assume that Frank dies on July 15, 2013. Frank's will establishes a trust for the benefit of his son, John. According to the terms of the trust, John is to receive the income from the trust each year. The remainderman of the trust is Frank's grandchild, Thomas. In addition, at his discretion,

Harry, the trustee of Frank's trust, may invade principal for John's health, education, maintenance, and support at any time. Assume that during the calendar year 2013, the net amount of ordinary income of the trust is $20,000. The ordinary income of the trust consists of dividend income and taxable interest income. The trust has no expenses for the year 2013. It has a short-term capital gain of $7,500 during the calendar year 2013. Harry, the trustee, invades principal on behalf of John to the extent of $5,000 in the year 2013.

Question: How much must John report with respect to his interest in Frank's trust on his Form 1040 for the calendar year 2013?

Answer: John will report on his Form 1040 for the calendar year 2013 the net ordinary income of the trust of $20,000 since the amount of the distributable net income of the trust is $20,000 for the year 2013. The $5,000 of principal that John receives during 2013 is tax-free to him. In general, capital gains are not included in the computation of distributable net income. The short-term capital gain of $7,500 is taxable to the trust for the year 2013 since it is not included in the computation of distributable net income. Under certain circumstances, capital gains could be included in the computation of distributable net income under the provisions of Frank's will.

An example taken from the Internal Revenue Service final regulations at Section 1.643(a)-3, on capital gains and losses, provides as follows:

Example 1

Under the terms of the Trust's governing instrument, all income is to be paid to A for life. [The] Trustee is given discretionary powers to invade principal for A's benefit and to deem discretionary distributions to be made from capital gains realized during the year. During [the] Trust's first taxable year, [the] Trust has $5,000 of dividend income and $10,000 of capital gain. . . . Pursuant to the terms of the governing instrument and applicable law, [the] Trustee allocates the $10,000 capital gain to principal. During the year [the] Trustee distributes to A $5,000 representing A's right to trust income. In addition, [the] Trustee distributes to A $12,000 pursuant to the discretionary power to invade principal. [The] Trustee does not exercise the discretionary power to deem the discretionary distributions as being paid from capital gains realized during the year. Therefore, the capital gains . . . are not included in distributable net income and the $10,000 of capital gain is taxed to the trust. In future years, [the] Trustee must treat all discretionary distributions as not being made from any realized capital gains.

Author's Note
I do not use the approach discussed in Example 1 for technical reasons.

Example 2
The facts are the same as in <u>Example 1</u> except that [the] Trustee intends to follow a regular practice of treating discretionary distributions of principal as being paid from any net capital gains realized by the Trust during the year. [The] Trustee evidences this treatment by including the $10,000 capital gain in distributable net income on the Trust's federal income tax return so that it is taxed to A. This treatment of capital gains is a reasonable exercise of [the] Trustee's discretion. In future years, [the] Trustee must treat all discretionary distributions as being made first from any realized capital gains.

Example 3
The facts are the same as in <u>Example 1</u> except that [the] Trustee intends to follow a regular practice of treating discretionary distributions as being paid from any net capital gains realized by [the] Trust during the year from the sale of certain specified assets or class of investments. This treatment is a reasonable exercise of [the] Trustee's discretion.

Example 4
The facts are the same as in <u>Example 1</u> except that pursuant to the terms of the governing instrument (in a provision not prohibited by applicable local law), capital gains realized by [the] Trust are allocated to income. Because the capital gains are allocated to income pursuant to the terms of the governing instrument, the $10,000

capital gain is included in [the] Trust's distributable net income for the taxable year.

DISTRIBUTABLE NET INCOME

Situation 40

Assume the facts in Situation 39 except that the trustee receives an annual trustee commission of $3,000 in 2013. Further assume that pursuant to the terms of the trust, all trustee commissions are charged to principal. Assume that the net ordinary income (accounting income) of the trust for the calendar year 2013 is still $20,000.

Question: How much must John report with respect to his interest in Frank's trust on his Form 1040 for the calendar year 2013?

Answer: John will report on his Form 1040 for the calendar year the net ordinary income of the trust, but only to the extent of $17,000. Although John receives net accounting income of $20,000 from the trust, he is taxable only to the extent of the distributable net income of the trust, or $17,000. The distributable net income rules for the IRS allow the annual trustee commissions of $3,000 to be deducted in the computation of distributable net income even though it is charged against principal. The deduction of $3,000 of trustee commissions should be allocated against the taxable interest income of the trust since dividends are taxed at a lower rate under the current law. In general, capital gains are not included in the computation of distributable net income.

Author's Note

In essence, through the mechanics of the computation of distributable net income, John is not taxed on $3,000 of the accounting income distribution of $20,000 that he receives from Frank's trust.

If the trust had received tax-exempt income, then a portion of the trustee commissions must be allocated to tax-exempt interest. According to the IRS, a pro rata portion of the trustee commission deduction is allocable to tax-exempt income.

Continued

Continued:

According to the IRS rules, the fact that the governing instrument or local law treats certain items that are payable from principal as a deduction for income tax purposes does not matter.

DISTRIBUTABLE NET INCOME

Situation 41

Assume the facts in Situation 40.

Question: Is the result described in Situation 40 fair to Thomas, the remainderman of the trust?

Answer: No. The remainderman of the trust is charged with the fiduciary income tax liability of the trust attributable to the short-term capital gain of $7,500. The remainderman does not obtain the benefit of the $3,000 tax deduction for the annual trustee commission, which is charged against principal. Since John, the income beneficiary of the trust, receives the benefit of the $3,000 tax deduction and Thomas, the remainderman, does not, Harry, the trustee, should make an equitable adjustment between income and principal because of this inequity. The authority for this equitable adjustment is EPTL 11-A-5.6. According to EPTL 11-A-5.6, a fiduciary may make an adjustment between principal and income to offset the shifting of economic interests or tax benefits between income beneficiaries and remainder beneficiaries that arise from an income tax or any other tax that is imposed upon the fiduciary or a beneficiary as a result of a transaction involving a distribution from the estate or trust.

DISTRIBUTABLE NET INCOME

Situation 42

Assume the facts in Situation 39. Also assume that the net amount of accounting income from Frank's trust for the calendar year 2013 is $20,000 and that the distributable net income for the calendar year 2013 is $20,000 as well. There are no annual trustee commissions for the calendar year 2013 because Harry, a close relative of John's, agrees to serve without trustee commissions. Harry, the trustee, invades principal to the extent of $5,000 during the calendar year 2013 for John because John needs the money for his support.

Question: How much must John report with respect to his interest in Frank's trust on his Form 1040 for the calendar year 2013?

Answer: John will report on his Form 1040 for the calendar year 2013 the net amount of accounting income of $20,000 since the distributable net income of the trust for the calendar year 2013 is $20,000. Although John receives $25,000 during the calendar year 2013, he is taxed only to the extent of $20,000, which is the amount of the distributable net income of the trust for the calendar year 2013. In general, capital gains are not included in the computation of distributable net income.

DISTRIBUTABLE NEW INCOME

Situation 43

Assume the facts in Situation 39. Also assume that Harry, the trustee, does not wish to invade principal on behalf of John because John does not need the additional $5,000 for his support. However, Harry agrees with John that based upon the fair market value of the trust assets as of January 2, 2013, John should receive an income distribution of approximately $25,000 for the calendar year 2013. Harry exercises his power to adjust and transfers $5,000 from principal to income pursuant to the authority granted to him under EPTL 11-2.3(b)(5) so that John receives $25,000 as an income distribution during the calendar year 2013. The distributable net income of the trust is $20,000 for the calendar year 2013. Harry does not take any annual trustee commissions. Remember that the trust has a short-term capital gain of $7,500 during the calendar year 2013.

Question: How much must John report with respect to his interest in Frank's trust on his Form 1040 for the calendar year 2013?

Answer: For the calendar year 2013, John will report on his Form 1040 the net ordinary income of $20,000 since the distributable net income of the trust is $20,000. Although John receives $25,000 as accounting income during the calendar year 2013, he is taxed only to the extent of $20,000, which is the amount of the distributable net income of the trust for the calendar year 2013. The fact that Harry, as trustee, transfers $5,000 from principal to income pursuant to his power to adjust under EPTL 11-2.3(b)(5) does not result in a change in the amount of the distributable net income of the trust for the calendar year 2013. The transfer from principal to income of $5,000 is under the power to adjust and does not change the tax-reporting position of the fiduciary income tax return of Frank's trust for the calendar year 2013. Further, in general, capital gains are not included in the computation of distributable net income.

DISTRIBUTABLE NET INCOME

Situation 44

Assume that Martin established a trust for the benefit of Carol under his will. Carol is to receive the income from the trust each year. The remainderman of the trust is his grandchild, Blake. Further assume that Martin dies on June 1, 2013. Paul, the trustee of Martin's trust, elects on August 1, 2013, that the optional unitrust provision under EPTL 11-2.4 shall be applicable to the trust as of January 1, 2014. As of January 2, 2014, the fair market value of the trust assets held in the trust is $1,000,000. During 2014, the trust has $15,000 of dividend income and $5,000 of taxable interest income. The trust has a short-term capital gain of $12,000 for the calendar year 2014. In addition, the annual trustee commissions paid to Paul in 2014 amount to $6,000, all of which is charged to principal under the terms of the trust.

Question: How much is the amount of the taxable distribution that Carol will receive for her interest in Martin's trust for the calendar year 2014?

Answer: Although Carol will receive a distribution of the unitrust amount of $40,000 (4 percent of $1,000,000) for her interest in Martin's trust for the calendar year 2014, she is not taxed on that amount. Carol's taxable distribution with respect to her interest in Martin's trust is limited to the amount of distributable net income. The distributable net income of Martin's trust for the calendar year 2014 is $14,000. The amount of the distributable net income is determined as follows:

Dividend income	$ 15,000
Interest income	5,000
Gross income	$ 20,000
Less: Trustee commissions	6,000
Distributable net income	$ 14,000

In essence, Carol receives a tax-free distribution of $26,000. This $26,000 amount is the difference between the unitrust payment amount and the amount of distributable net income ($40,000 – $14,000).

DISTRIBUTABLE NET INCOME

Situation 45
Assume the facts in Situation 44.

Question: How much is the taxable income of the trust for the calendar year 2014?

Answer: $11,700. This is computed as follows:

Dividend income		$15,000
Interest income		5,000
Short-term capital gain		12,000
Gross income		$32,000
Less: Trustee commissions	$ 6,000	
*Distribution deduction	14,000	
Personal exemption	300	
Total deductions		20,300
Taxable income of trust		$11,700

*Although Carol receives a unitrust distribution of $40,000 as the income beneficiary of the trust for the taxable year 2014, she is taxed only to the extent of $14,000, the distributable net income of the trust for the calendar year 2014. The taxable income of the trust is composed of the following:

Short-term capital gain	$12,000
Less: Personal exemption	3,000
Taxable income of trust	$11,700

The distribution deduction is limited to the amount of distributable net income.

Author's Note

In the event that the optional unitrust provision is applicable to the trust, the UPAIA is not applicable to the trust. Therefore, Paul, as trustee, may not make an equitable adjustment between income and principal to account for the fact that Carol receives the tax benefit of the trustee commission deduction of $6,000. Therefore, the remainderman of the trust is charged with the trustee commissions of $6,000 that are paid by the trustee. In addition, the remainderman of the trust is charged with the income tax liability attributable to the short-term capital gain of the trust and does not receive any tax benefit for the trustee commissions that are charged against principal. There is no provision under the unitrust rules for an equitable adjustment between income and principal.

APPENDIX A

UNIFORM TRUST CODE

The Uniform Trust Code (UTC) was approved by the National Conference of Commissioners on Uniform State Laws in 2000 and has been amended several times thereafter.

It is an attempt by the commissioners to cover details involved in the rise of the administration of trusts in the United States. A state (including the District of Columbia) may adopt in whole or in part versions of the suggested provisions adopted by the commissioners. However, a state need not adopt the recommendations of the commissioners.

The purpose of the UTC is to attempt to codify the law of trusts, because the commission recognizes that many individuals use trusts in estate planning. It is an attempt to provide uniformity to the trust laws and cover many issues that need to be clarified and that often come up with respect to the administration of trusts.

The recommended provisions by the commissioners are default rules that apply if the trust document fails to address a particular issue.

The UTC provisions are extremely detailed and cover many issues. A sample state that has adopted a version of the UTC has been selected to show the extent of the coverage of the UTC. The sample state is Florida, and the categories of coverage are shown below.

Chapter 736, Florida Trust Code

Part I
General Provisions and Definitions
    736.0101   Short title

Part II
Judicial Proceedings

Part III
Representation

Part IV
Creation, Validity, Modification and Termination

Part V
Creditors' Claims; Spendthrift and Discretionary Trusts

Part XI
Rules of Construction

Part XII
Charitable Trusts

Part XIII
Miscellaneous

It should be noted that the Florida Trust Code is generally effective on July 1, 2007, and applies to all trusts created before, on, or after July 1, 2007.

The Florida Trust Code follows the provisions of the UTC to a major extent. However, Florida law modifies and adds certain provisions to its version.

As you can see, a trustee has a significant degree of responsibility. The trustee may not know the rules that apply to him or her in administering a trust under the UTC trust laws of the particular jurisdiction that is applicable. Being a trustee is an important position since the trustee must know the rules or be advised as to the responsibility.

Over 20 states plus the District of Columbia have adopted some version of the UTC.

Here are a few selected provisions of the Florida Trust Code.

736.0306   Designated representative.—

(1) If specifically nominated in the trust instrument, one or more persons may be designated to represent and bind a beneficiary and receive any notice, information, accounting, or report. The trust instrument may also authorize any person or persons, other than a trustee of the trust, to designate one or more persons to represent

and bind a beneficiary and receive any notice, information, accounting, or report.

(2) Except as otherwise provided in this code, a person designated, as provided in subsection (1) may not represent and bind a beneficiary while that person is serving as trustee.

(3) Except as otherwise provided in this code, a person designated, as provided in subsection (1) may not represent and bind another beneficiary if the person designated also is a beneficiary, unless:

   (a) That person was named by the settlor; or

   (b) That person is the beneficiary's spouse or a grandparent or descendant of a grandparent of the beneficiary or the beneficiary's spouse.

   (c) No person designated, as provided in subsection (1), is liable to the beneficiary whose interests are represented, or to anyone claiming through that beneficiary, for any actions or omissions to act made in good faith.

History.—s. 3, ch. 2006-217; s. 4, ch. 2009-117.

736.05055   Notice of trust.—

(1) Upon the death of a settlor of a trust described in s. 733.707(3), the trustee must file a notice of trust with the court of the county of the settlor's domicile and the court having jurisdiction of the settlor's estate.

(2) The notice of trust must contain the name of the settlor, the settlor's date of death, the title of the trust, if any, the date of the trust, and the name and address of the trustee.

(3) If the settlor's probate proceeding has been commenced, the clerk shall notify the trustee in writing of the date of the commencement of the probate proceeding and the file number.

(4) The clerk shall file and index the notice of trust in the same manner as a caveat unless there exists a probate proceeding for the settlor's estate, in which case the notice of trust must be filed in the probate proceeding and the clerk shall send a copy to the personal representative.

(5) The clerk shall send a copy of any caveat filed regarding the settlor to the trustee, and the notice of trust to any caveator, unless there is a probate proceeding pending and the personal representative and the trustee are the same.

(6) Any proceeding affecting the expenses of the administration or obligations of the settlor's estate prior to the trustee filing a notice of trust are binding on the trustee.

(7) The trustee's failure to file the notice of trust does not affect the trustee's obligation to pay expenses of administration and obligations of the settlor's estate as provided in s.733.607(2).

History.—s. 5, ch. 2006-217.

736.0705   Resignation of trustee.—

(1) A trustee may resign:
   (a) Upon at least 30 days' notice to the qualified beneficiaries, the settlor, if living, and all cotrustees; or
   (b) With the approval of the court.

(2) In approving a resignation, the court may issue orders and impose conditions reasonably necessary for the protection of the trust property.

(3) Any liability of a resigning trustee or of any sureties on the trustee's bond for acts or omissions of the trustee is not discharged or affected by the trustee's resignation.

History.—s. 7, ch. 2006-217.

736.0706   Removal of trustee.—

(1) The settlor, a cotrustee, or a beneficiary may request the court to remove a trustee, or a trustee may be removed by the court on the court's own initiative.

(2) The court may remove a trustee if:
   (a) The trustee has committed a serious breach of trust;
   (b) The lack of cooperation among cotrustees substantially impairs the administration of the trust;
   (c) Due to the unfitness, unwillingness, or persistent failure of the trustee to administer the trust effectively, the court determines

that removal of the trustee best serves the interests of the beneficiaries; or

(d) There has been a substantial change of circumstances or removal is requested by all of the qualified beneficiaries, the court finds that removal of the trustee best serves the interests of all of the beneficiaries and is not inconsistent with a material purpose of the trust, and a suitable cotrustee or successor trustee is available.

(3) Pending a final decision on a request to remove a trustee, or in lieu of or in addition to removing a trustee, the court may order such appropriate relief under s. 736.1001(2) as may be necessary to protect the trust property or the interests of the beneficiaries.

History.—s. 7, ch. 2006-217.

736.0708   Compensation of trustee.—

(1) If the terms of a trust do not specify the trustee's compensation, a trustee is entitled to compensation that is reasonable under the circumstances.

(2) If the terms of a trust specify the trustee's compensation, the trustee is entitled to be compensated as specified, but the court may allow more or less compensation if:

(a) The duties of the trustee are substantially different from those contemplated when the trust was created; or

(b) The compensation specified by the terms of the trust would be unreasonably low or high.

(3) If the trustee has rendered other services in connection with the administration of the trust, the trustee shall also be allowed reasonable compensation for the other services rendered in addition to reasonable compensation as trustee.

History.—s. 7, ch. 2006-217.

736.0813   Duty to inform and account.—The trustee shall keep the qualified beneficiaries of the trust reasonably informed of the trust and its administration.

(1) The trustee's duty to inform and account includes, but is not limited to, the following:

   (a) Within 60 days after acceptance of the trust, the trustee shall give notice to the qualified beneficiaries of the acceptance of the trust, the full name and address of the trustee, and that the fiduciary lawyer-client privilege in s. 90.5021 applies with respect to the trustee and any attorney employed by the trustee.

   (b) Within 60 days after the date the trustee acquires knowledge of the creation of an irrevocable trust, or the date the trustee acquires knowledge that a formerly revocable trust has become irrevocable, whether by the death of the settlor or otherwise, the trustee shall give notice to the qualified beneficiaries of the trust's existence, the identity of the settlor or settlors, the right to request a copy of the trust instrument, the right to accountings under this section, and that the fiduciary lawyer-client privilege in s. 90.5021 applies with respect to the trustee and any attorney employed by the trustee.

   (c) Upon reasonable request, the trustee shall provide a qualified beneficiary with a complete copy of the trust instrument.

   (d) A trustee of an irrevocable trust shall provide a trust accounting, as set forth in s. 736.08135, from the date of the last accounting or, if none, from the date on which the trustee became accountable, to each qualified beneficiary at least annually and on termination of the trust or on change of the trustee.

   (e) Upon reasonable request, the trustee shall provide a qualified beneficiary with relevant information about the assets and liabilities of the trust and the particulars relating to administration. Paragraphs (a) and (b) do not apply to an irrevocable trust created before the effective date of this code, or to a revocable trust that becomes irrevocable before the effective date of this code. Paragraph (a) does not apply to a trustee who accepts a trusteeship before the effective date of this code.

(2) A qualified beneficiary may waive the trustee's duty to account under paragraph (1)(d). A qualified beneficiary may withdraw a waiver previously given. Waivers and withdrawals of prior waivers under this subsection must be in writing. Withdrawals of prior waivers are effective only with respect to accountings for future periods.

(3) The representation provisions of part III apply with respect to all rights of a qualified beneficiary under this section.

(4) As provided in s. 736.0603(1), the trustee's duties under this section extend only to the settlor while a trust is revocable.

(5) This section applies to trust accountings rendered for accounting periods beginning on or after July 1, 2007.

History.—s. 8, ch. 2006-217; s. 15, ch. 2007-153; s. 11, ch. 2011-183; s. 14, ch. 2013-172.

736.08135   Trust accountings.—

(1) A trust accounting must be a reasonably understandable report from the date of the last accounting or, if none, from the date on which the trustee became accountable, that adequately discloses the information required in subsection (2).

(2)

(a) The accounting must begin with a statement identifying the trust, the trustee furnishing the accounting, and the time period covered by the accounting.

(b) The accounting must show all cash and property transactions and all significant transactions affecting administration during the accounting period, including compensation paid to the trustee and the trustee's agents. Gains and losses realized during the accounting period and all receipts and disbursements must be shown.

(c) To the extent feasible, the accounting must identify and value trust assets on hand at the close of the accounting period. For each asset or class of assets reasonably capable of valuation, the accounting shall contain two values, the asset acquisition value or carrying value and the estimated current value. The accounting must identify each known noncontingent liability with an estimated current amount of the liability if known.

(d) To the extent feasible, the accounting must show significant transactions that do not affect the amount for which the trustee is accountable, including name changes in investment holdings, adjustments to carrying value, a change of custodial institutions, and stock splits.

(e) The accounting must reflect the allocation of receipts, disbursements, accruals, or allowances between income and principal when the allocation affects the interest of any beneficiary of the trust.

(f) The trustee shall include in the final accounting a plan of distribution for any undistributed assets shown on the final accounting.

(3) This section applies to all trust accountings rendered for any accounting periods beginning on or after January 1, 2003.

History.—s. 8, ch. 2006-217.

736.1001 Remedies for breach of trust.—

(1) A violation by a trustee of a duty the trustee owes to a beneficiary is a breach of trust.

(2) To remedy a breach of trust that has occurred or may occur, the court may:

(a) Compel the trustee to perform the trustee's duties;

(b) Enjoin the trustee from committing a breach of trust;

(c) Compel the trustee to redress a breach of trust by paying money or restoring property or by other means;

(d) Order a trustee to account;

(e) Appoint a special fiduciary to take possession of the trust property and administer the trust;

(f) Suspend the trustee;

(g) Remove the trustee as provided in s. 736.0706;

(h) Reduce or deny compensation to the trustee;

(i) Subject to s. 736.1016, void an act of the trustee, impose a lien or a constructive trust on trust property, or trace trust property wrongfully disposed of and recover the property or its proceeds; or

(j) Order any other appropriate relief.

(3) As an illustration of the remedies available to the court and without limiting the court's discretion as provided in subsection (2), if a breach of trust results in the favoring of any beneficiary to the detriment of any other beneficiary or consists of an abuse of the trustee's discretion:

    (a) To the extent the breach of trust has resulted in no distribution to a beneficiary or a distribution that is too small, the court may require the trustee to pay from the trust to the beneficiary an amount the court determines will restore the beneficiary, in whole or in part, to his or her appropriate position.

    (b) To the extent the breach of trust has resulted in a distribution to a beneficiary that is too large, the court may restore the beneficiaries, the trust, or both, in whole or in part, to their appropriate positions by requiring the trustee to withhold an amount from one or more future distributions to the beneficiary who received the distribution that was too large or by requiring that beneficiary to return some or all of the distribution to the trust.

History.—s. 10, ch. 2006-217; s. 147, ch. 2007-5; s. 19, ch. 2007-153.

APPENDIX B

UNIFORM PRINCIPAL AND INCOME ACT

Most states have adopted a version of the Uniform Principal and Income Act (UPAIA) promulgated by the National Conference of Commissioners in 1997 and amended in 2008. These rules for the most part cover trust accounting income and principles that apply to trusts.

A sample state that has adopted a version of the UPAIA has been selected to show the extent of the average UPAIA. Please be aware that Florida's version of the UPAIA is not the same as New York's version of the UPAIA, for example. The sample state is Florida, and the categories of coverage are shown below.

2013 FLORIDA STATUTES, CHAPTER 738

Principal and Income

APPENDIX C

A UNITRUST COURT CASE IN NEW YORK STATE

In Re Heller
COURT OF APPEALS OF NEW YORK
(6 N.Y.3d 649; 849 N.E.2d 262; 816 N.Y.S.2d 403)
May 4, 2006

Summary of In re Heller, a New York Court of Appeals Case Regarding Unitrust Trusts

In re Heller resolves the issues of whether an interested trustee is prohibited from making a trust a unitrust, and whether a trustee may apply a unitrust election retroactively. In In re Heller, the appellant sought to have a retroactive unitrust election annulled. The trustees made the unitrust election in March 2003 and applied it retroactively to January 1, 2002, the date on which unitrust provision [for this trust] became effective. The appellant argued that the trustees were prohibited from making the trust a unitrust because of their status as interested trustees. The appellant also argued that the unitrust election could not be applied retroactively to the effective date of the unitrust provision [for this trust]. The New York Court of Appeals affirmed the Appellate Division's ruling that an interested trustee is not prohibited simply by his status as an interested trustee from making a trust a unitrust and that a trustee may choose to apply the unitrust election retroactively to the effective date of the unitrust provision [for this trust].

The case follows:

In re Heller

IN RE: Jacob HELLER, Deceased.   Sandra Davis, as Attorney-in-Fact for Bertha M. Heller, Appellant; Herbert M. Miller et al., Respondents.

—May 04, 2006

Greenfield Stein & Senior, LLP, New York City (Gary B. Freidman and Jeffery H. Sheetz of counsel), for appellant, Thacher Proffitt & Wood LLP, White Plains (Kevin J. Plunkett, Darius P. Chafizadeh and Stefanie A. Bashar of counsel), and Greenberg Traurig, LLP, New York City (Linda B. Hirschson of counsel), for respondents.

OPINION OF THE COURT

In September 2001, New York enacted legislation that transformed the definition and treatment of trust accounting income. The Uniform Principal and Income Act (EPTL art. 11-A) and related statutes (L. 2001, ch. 243), including the optional unitrust provision (EPTL 11-2.4), are designed to facilitate investment for total return on a portfolio. The appeal before us centers on the optional unitrust provision, which permits trustees to elect a regime in which income is calculated according to a fixed formula and based on the net fair market value of the trust assets. We hold that a trustee's status as a remainder beneficiary does not in itself invalidate a unitrust election made by that trustee, and that a trustee may elect unitrust status retroactively to January 1, 2002, the effective date of EPTL 11-2.4.

I.

In his will, after making certain other gifts of personal property and money, Jacob Heller created a trust to benefit his wife Bertha Heller (should she survive him) and his children. Heller provided that his entire residuary estate be held in trust during Bertha's life. He appointed his brother Frank Heller as trustee and designated his sons Herbert and Alan Heller as trustees on Frank's death. Every year Bertha was to receive the greater of $40,000 or the total income of the trust. Heller named his daughters

(Suzanne Heller and Faith Willinger, each with a 30% share) and his sons and prospective trustees (Herbert and Alan Heller, each with a 20% share) as remainder beneficiaries.

Jacob Heller died in 1986, and his wife Bertha survives him. When Heller's brother Frank died in 1997, Herbert and Alan Heller became trustees. From that year until 2001, Bertha Heller received an average annual income from the trust of approximately $190,000. In March 2003, the trustees elected to have the unitrust provision apply, pursuant to EPTL 11-2.4(e)(1)(B)(I). As required by EPTL 11-2.4(e)(1)(B)(III), they notified trust beneficiaries Bertha Heller, Suzanne Heller and Faith Willinger. The trustees sought to have unitrust treatment applied retroactively to January 1, 2002, the effective date of EPTL 11-2.4. As a result of that election, Bertha Heller's annual income was reduced to approximately $70,000.

Appellant Sandra Davis commenced this proceeding, as attorney-in-fact for her mother Bertha Heller, and on August 1, 2003 moved for summary judgment, seeking, among other things, an order annulling the unitrust election and revoking the letters of trusteeship issued to Herbert and Alan Heller. She also sought a determination that the election could not be made retroactive to January 1, 2002. Surrogate's Court granted the branch of her summary judgment motion that sought to void the trustees' retroactive application of the unitrust election, but denied the branches of her motion seeking annulment of the unitrust election itself and other relief.

Davis appealed Surrogate's Court's order, and Herbert and Alan Heller cross-appealed. The Appellate Division affirmed the order to the extent that it denied Davis's summary judgment motion and reversed so much of the order as annulled the retroactive application of the unitrust election. It also granted leave to appeal and certified the following question to us: "Was the opinion and order of [the Appellate Division] dated August 15, 2005, properly made?" We conclude that it was and now affirm.

II.

The 2001 legislation that forms the subject of this appeal was designed to make it easier for trustees to comply with the demands of the Prudent Investor Act of 1994.[1] In addition to enacting EPTL article 11-A (Uniform Principal and Income Act), the Legislature both added EPTL

11-2.3(b)(5) to the Prudent Investor Act and included the optional uni-trust provision, EPTL 11-2.4.

Under the former Principal and Income Act (EPTL 11-2.1),2 a trustee was required to balance the interests of the income beneficiary against those of the remainder beneficiary (see EPTL 11-2.1[a][1]), and was constrained in making investments by the act's narrow definitions of income and principal (see EPTL 11-2.1[b]). A trustee who invested in nonappreciating assets would ensure reasonable income for any income beneficiary, but would sacrifice growth opportunities for the trust funds, as inflation eroded their value; if the trustee invested for growth, remainder beneficiaries would enjoy an increase in the value of the trust at the expense of income beneficiaries.3 Moreover, the need to invest so as to produce what the former Principal and Income Act defined as income led to investment returns that failed to represent the benefits envisaged as appropriate by settlors.4

The Prudent Investor Act encourages investing for total return on a portfolio. Unless the governing instrument expressly provides otherwise, the act requires that trustees "pursue an overall investment strategy to enable the trustee to make appropriate present and future distributions to or for the benefit of the beneficiaries under the governing instrument, in accordance with risk and return objectives reasonably suited to the entire portfolio" (EPTL 11-2.3[b][3][A] [emphasis added]).

The 2001 legislation allows trustees to pursue this strategy uninhibited by a constrained concept of trust accounting income. First, the Prudent Investor Act now authorizes trustees "to adjust between principal and income to the extent the trustee considers advisable to enable the trustee to make appropriate present and future distributions in accordance with clause (b)(3)(A) if the trustee determines, after applying the rules in article 11-A, that such an adjustment would be fair and reasonable to all of the beneficiaries, so that current beneficiaries may be given such use of the trust property as is consistent with preservation of its value" (EPTL 11-2.3[b][5] [A]).

A trustee investing for a portfolio's total return under the Prudent Investor Act may now adjust principal and income to compensate for the effects of the investment decisions on distribution to income beneficiaries (see 14 Warren's Heaton, Surrogates' Courts, at App 5-25-5-27). Alternatively, the optional unitrust provision lets trustees elect unitrust status for a trust (EPTL 11-2.4), by which income is calculated according to a fixed formula.

In a unitrust pursuant to EPTL 11-2.4, an income beneficiary receives an annual income distribution of "four percent of the net fair market values of the assets held in the trust on the first business day of the current valuation year" (EPTL 11-2.4[b][1]), for the first three years of unitrust treatment. This is true regardless of the actual income earned by the trust. Starting in the fourth year, the value of the trust assets is determined by calculating the average of three figures: the net fair market value on the first business day of the current valuation year and the net fair market values on the first business days of the prior two valuation years (see EPTL 11-2.4 [b][2]). Income generated in excess of this amount is applied to principal.

Under the 2001 legislation, then, a trustee may invest in assets, such as equities, that outperform other types of investment in the long term but produce relatively low dividend yields for an income beneficiary, and still achieve impartial treatment of income and remainder beneficiaries. The trustee may accomplish this either by adjusting as between principal and income (see 14 Warren's Heaton, Surrogates' Courts, at App. 5-25-5-27) or by electing unitrust status with the result that the income increases in proportion to the value of the principal (id. at App. 5-14). If a trust's assets are primarily interests in nonappreciating investments producing high yields for income beneficiaries, a unitrust election may initially result in a substantial decrease in the distribution to any income beneficiary, at least until the portfolio is diversified. This case presents such a scenario.

III.

Davis argues that the trustees are barred as a matter of law from electing unitrust status because they are themselves remainder beneficiaries, and that, in any case, they may not elect unitrust status retroactively to January 1, 2002. The Appellate Division held that the legislation does not impede unitrust election by an interested trustee, that such an election is not inconsistent, per se, with common-law limitations on the conduct of fiduciaries and that the statute permits trustees to select retroactive application. We agree.

EPTL 11-2.3(b)(5), the 2001 statute that gives trustees the power to adjust between principal and income, expressly prohibits a trustee from exercising this power if "the trustee is a current beneficiary or a presumptive remainderman of the trust" (EPTL 11-2.3[b][5] [C][vii]) or if "the adjustment would benefit the trustee directly or indirectly" (EPTL 11-2.3[b] [5][C] [viii]). Tellingly, the Legislature included no such prohibition in the simultaneously enacted optional unitrust provision, EPTL 11-2.4. Moreover, in giving a list of factors to be considered by the courts in determining whether unitrust treatment should apply to a trust, the Legislature mentioned no absolute prohibitions (see EPTL 11-2.4[e][5][A]), and created a presumption in favor of unitrust application (EPTL 11-2.4[e][5][B]). We conclude that the Legislature did not mean to prohibit trustees who have a beneficial interest from electing unitrust treatment.

It is certainly true that the common law in New York contains an absolute prohibition against self-dealing, in that "a fiduciary owes a duty of undivided and undiluted loyalty to those whose interests the fiduciary is to protect" (Birnbaum v. Birnbaum, 73 N.Y.2d 461, 466, 541 N.Y.S.2d 746, 539 N.E.2d 574 [1989]). "The trustee is under a duty to the beneficiary to administer the trust solely in the interest of the beneficiary" (Restatement [Second] of Trusts § 170[1]). In this case, however, the trustees owe fiduciary obligations not only to the trust's income beneficiary, Bertha Heller, but also to the other remainder beneficiaries, Suzanne Heller and Faith Willinger. That these beneficiaries' interests happen to align with the trustees' does not relieve the trustees of their duties to them. Here, we cannot conclude that the trustees are prohibited from electing unitrust treatment as a matter of common-law principle.

That the trustees are remainder beneficiaries does not, by itself, invalidate a unitrust election. Nevertheless, a unitrust election from which a trustee benefits will be scrutinized by the courts with special care. In determining whether application of the optional unitrust provision is appropriate, it remains for the Surrogate to review the process and assure the fairness of the trustees' election, by applying relevant factors including those enumerated in EPTL 11-2.4(e)(5)(A). Application of these factors here presents questions of fact precluding summary judgment.

IV.

Davis seeks to reinstate Surrogate's Court's determination that the unitrust election could not be made retroactive to January 1, 2002. In our view, however, the Legislature structured EPTL 11-2.4 so that it could be applied retroactively. EPTL 11-2.4(d) (1) provides that a trustee who elects unitrust status may specify the date on which the interest of a beneficiary begins. Thus, the statute vests trustees with authority to determine the effective date of unitrust elections.

Moreover, EPTL 11-2.4(b)(6) instructs a trustee who elects unitrust treatment to "determine the unitrust amount properly payable for any preceding and current valuation year of the trust" (emphasis added), unless the election is "expressly made effective prospectively as permitted under clause (e)(4)(a)." The trustee is then required to pay to, or recover from, the current beneficiary the difference between the unitrust amount and any amount actually paid for any completed valuation year. (EPTL 11-2.4[b] [6].) This provision envisages retroactive application of a unitrust regime. The required recomputation of preceding years' beneficial interests would serve no purpose if retroactive application were barred.

EPTL 11-2.4(e)(4)(A), on which Surrogate's Court relied, is not to the contrary This section provides that the optional unitrust provision "shall apply to a trust as of the first year of the trust in which assets first become subject to the trust, unless the governing instrument or the court in its decision provides otherwise, or unless the election in accordance with clause (e)(1)(B) is expressly made effective as of the first day of the first year of the trust commencing after the election is made."

On the most plausible interpretation of this less than lucid provision, EPTL 11-2.4(e)(4)(A) actually contemplates retroactivity, insofar as it provides the initial funding of the trust as a default starting point for unitrust treatment of a trust created on or after January 1, 2002. Certainly, EPTL 11-2.4(e)(4) (A) should not be read as taking away from trustees the authority given them by EPTL 11-2.4(d)(1) to specify the effective date of a unitrust election.

We therefore hold that a trustee may elect unitrust status for a trust retroactively to January 1, 2002, the effective date of EPTL 11-2.4. Appellant's remaining contentions lack merit.

Accordingly, the order of the Appellate Division should be affirmed, with costs, and the certified question answered in the affirmative.

Order affirmed, etc.

FOOTNOTES

1. See e.g. Legis. Mem. in Support of 5th Report of EPTL-SCPA Legis Advisory Comm., 14 Warren's Heaton, Surrogates' Courts, Appendix 5.03, at App 5-171 (6th ed. rev.).

2. The former Principal and Income Act (EPTL 11-2.1) was superseded by the Uniform Principal and Income Act (EPTL art. 11-A) enacted in 2001. The former act does not apply to receipts and expenses received or incurred after January 1, 2002 (EPTL 11-2.1[m]).

3. See Turano, Practice Commentaries, McKinney's Cons. Laws of N.Y., Book 17B, EPTL art. 11-A, 2006 Pocket Part, at 82-83; see also 5th Report of EPTL-SCPA Legis Advisory Comm., 14 Warren's Heaton, Surrogates' Courts, Appendix 5.01, at App. 5-4-5-13 (6th ed. rev.).

4. See 14 Warren's Heaton, Surrogates' Courts, at App. 5-4-5-5.

ROSENBLATT, J.

Chief Judge KAYE and Judges G.B. SMITH, CIPARICK, GRAFFEO, READ and R.S. SMITH concur.

Limited Quick
Reference Glossary

Distributable net income: This is an IRS rule that is used in order to determine the amount of income that a trust beneficiary must report. A trust accountant should know how to calculate the amount that the trust beneficiary must report. The trust accountant must become familiar with the provisions of the trust document and the UPAIA rules in the particular jurisdiction.

Living trust scams: These involve sales pitches of canned agreements to senior citizens by salespeople who are interested in selling products to them. I have run into this situation recently, and it was a nightmare that involved many product sales and a canned book of trusts.

Power to adjust: Many trust accounting laws allow the trustee to transfer principal to income or vice versa to make sure that the trust beneficiary who is an income beneficiary receives a reasonable amount of income. The reason for the rule is that if the trustee invests substantially in equities, then the trust income beneficiary may receive only a negligible amount of income. In that case, the trustee can transfer a reasonable amount of principal to income during the accounting period to enhance the amount that the trustee income beneficiary receives with respect to a given year.

Remedies for breach of trust: If a trustee violates his or her duty as a trustee, then the trustee can be removed, lose his or her trustee compensation, and/or be held personally liable for any damages and may have to pay for his or her legal defense fees personally.

Statute of limitations: The statute of limitations means the time in which a proceeding may be commenced against a trustee. It is based on the law of the particular jurisdiction. The statute of limitations may be extensive in a particular jurisdiction.

Trust accountings: A trustee may have to do an extensive accounting when the trust is terminated. This can be time consuming and costly as well. A trustee must keep good records and account for his or her actions during his or her tenure. If the trustee becomes disabled or dies, then the legal representative of the trustee must account to the trust beneficiaries in the absence of a release by the trust beneficiaries.

Uniform Principal and Income Act (UPAIA): The UPAIA covers what is income and principal from a trust administration point of view. Most states have adopted versions of the UPAIA with various effective dates. These rules apply unless the trust agreement specifically provides that certain provisions do not apply. The trustee is responsible for knowing what is considered to be income and/or principal in the jurisdiction that controls the interpretation of the trust document. The trust accounting rules are modified from time to time. Some of the UPAIA rules are largely mandatory, and others are discretionary. A trust attorney and a trust accountant should know the rules and explain them to both the grantor and the trustee. Most states over the last 15 years or more have completely revamped their trust accounting rules. A state for this purpose also includes the District of Columbia. Over 40 jurisdictions have adopted versions of the UPAIA.

Uniform Trust Code (UTC): The UTC covers many technical issues that come up in the administration of a trust other than the trust accounting income and principal rules. A number of jurisdictions have adopted versions of the UTC with various effective dates. Many more jurisdictions have adopted the UPAIA than have adopted the UTC. The UTC is detailed, and the trustee must be made aware of the rules that apply in his or her jurisdiction if the trust is subject to the UTC. Over 20 jurisdictions have adopted versions of the UTC. The trust attorney will advise the trustee as to the rules.

Unitrust: Many states provide that a trust may be administered as a unitrust. In essence, the trust income beneficiary receives a fixed percentage of the assets in the trust. This may be a reasonable way of satisfying the distributions to a trust income beneficiary if most of the trust assets are held in equities that produce a negligible amount of income.

Index